Main Street, Not Wall Street

MAIN STREET, NOT WALL STREET

INVESTING CLOSE TO HOME—
THE SMART WAY TO MAKE
MORE MONEY

John Rubino

William Morrow and Company, Inc.
New York

Copyright © 1998 by John Rubino

It is the policy of William Morrow and Company, Inc., and its imprints and affiliates,
recognizing the importance of preserving what has been written, to print the books
we publish on acid-free paper, and we exert our best efforts to that end.

Library of Congress Cataloging-in-Publication Data

Rubino, John A.
    Main street, not Wall Street : investing close to home : the smart way to make more
money / John Rubino. — 1st ed.
        p.   cm.
    Includes bibliographical references.
    ISBN 0-688-15421-2
    1. Investments.   2. Stocks.   I. Title
HG4521.R783   1998
332.63'22—dc21   97-47694
                                                                                CIP

Printed in the United States of America

First Edition

1   2   3   4   5   6   7   8   9   10

BOOK DESIGN BY BERNARD KLEIN

www.williammorrow.com

For April

CONTENTS

INTRODUCTION

If you are like most people, your financial life is divided into two distinct parts. One contains your paycheck and your home, the value of which depend on the health of the local economy. That's the Main Street side.

The other side contains your investments, which consist mostly of established mutual funds and brand-name stocks, accumulated on the advice of the major brokerage houses, mutual fund companies and financial publications. Call this the Wall Street side.

Conventional wisdom approves of this division. After all, you're the expert on your job and your home, and you should handle them. Wall Street is adept at managing money, populated as it is by people with the brains, connections and resources to stay one step ahead of a changing world. So Merrill Lynch, Fidelity and *The Wall Street Journal* are your best sources of investment ideas.

This is perfectly logical. But it's also increasingly wrong: Professional money managers, as a group, have consistently failed to generate returns high enough to justify their fees. And Main Street, in just the past few years, has become an extraordinarily good source of market-beating investments. In most metropolitan areas, a boom in initial public offerings is creating a whole new generation of emerging growth stocks, and it's doing it far too quickly for out-of-town money managers to keep up. Meanwhile, coalescing around these swarms of newborn companies are *local* investment communities, made up of the following:

- Local business journals, which serve as mini–*Wall Street Journals* with a focus on one metropolitan area;
- Regional brokerage houses and investment banks, which specialize in the stocks of a single city or region;
- Venture capital clubs, which bring together people interested in investing in and working with emerging local companies;
- Investment clubs made up of people who pool their connections and knowledge of the local business scene to find promising companies nearby;
- Individual investors who have realized that their fortunes are best sought close to home.

Together, they form a kind of Wall Street in microcosm, with two big differences: The ideas they're generating really can help you beat the market, and their ideas are readily available—if you know where to look and how to ask.

I began to form the idea for this book in 1991, after spending a decade on the real Wall Street, analyzing stocks for the *The Value Line Investment Survey* and junk bonds for a couple of mutual funds. My wife, April—also a financial analyst—and I had saved enough money to let us trade the quick and dirty life of Manhattan for something slower, cleaner and greener, and we'd chosen a nice little piece of rural suburbia near Richmond, Virginia. Soon I found myself writing for several magazines, among them *Virginia Business*, a statewide magazine that wanted a monthly column on Virginia stocks.

This column had a twist that was both intriguing and disturbing: Both the stocks profiled and the corroborating sources had to come from within the state. I accepted the assignment, though frankly I doubted that a medium-sized state like Virginia would yield more than a few months' worth of interesting ideas.

Was I ever wrong. Virginia turned out to be home to more than a hundred public companies of every conceivable kind. Big, small, high-tech, low-tech, brand-new IPOs and old-line blue chips. And new local companies were going public faster than I was able to work through the existing stories. Just as important, there were dozens of local people who knew these companies well and were willing to talk about them.

These "local experts" worked for organizations that I hadn't known existed: They were analysts at local and regional brokerage houses, reporters at local business journals and assorted other movers and shakers who were connected in one way or another to the business communities of Richmond, Alexandria and Norfolk. They helped local entrepreneurs build new companies and take them public. They wrote about these companies' progress, peddled their stocks to clients and helped them secure expansion capital. In short, they knew many of these companies better and sooner than just about anyone else.

Before long I was turning up some extraordinary pieces of information, the kind of semi-insider stuff that I seldom saw on

Wall Street. "Yeah," some analyst would tell me, "I'm the only one that covers XYZ Corp. I had dinner with the CEO last week and he says they'll grow by sixty percent this year and their earnings will double. The stock price is down since the IPO because it's too illiquid for most institutions, but we're putting our retail clients into it."

Or another new acquaintance would offer matter-of-factly: "You should write about ABC, Inc. I have a friend who programs computers for them and he says their new division is making so much money that they're looking for ways to hide it from the government."

Then there were the press releases put out by small companies that had just gotten major orders, and the newspaper articles quoting some local company's chairman in detail about his plans. Almost daily, I was putting down the phone and muttering, "Damn, I wish I'd heard about this back when."

Eventually, it dawned on me that I was working with a different *category* of information, which had been released and picked up locally but not nationally, primarily because it concerned companies that were generally too small, new or remote to have caught Wall Street's eye. Virginians who paid attention to their local papers, traded through a local brokerage house and listened to their friends had a chance to become the real experts on the twenty, thirty or fifty stocks within their part of the state.

Then, gradually, an even more interesting notion began to take shape: As the 1990s progressed, the sources I was tapping seemed to be coalescing into a local investing *infrastructure*, an identifiable community of people and organizations dedicated to nurturing, reporting on and investing in nearby emerging companies. By plugging into this network, I was, in effect, joining a team made up of dozens of smart people who were way ahead of Wall Street when it came to this small universe of stocks.

To test this thesis, I created a newsletter, *The Main Street Report*, to collect the ideas of successful local investors in other places. By offering them a little out-of-town publicity, I was able to wrangle free subscriptions from business journals in other cities and copies of research from local and regional brokerage houses. Out-of-state analysts even returned my calls. Soon I had access to the same kinds of not-yet-widely-known skinny on emerging growth stocks from Portland to Dallas to Boston. And it became clear that just about any good-sized metropolitan area now has a network of local investing expertise, and that anyone can tap into it with a few simple steps.

On Peter Lynch

The idea that you should invest in things you understand has been around forever, but it took a quantum leap toward respectability when Peter Lynch published *One Up on Wall Street* in 1989. Lynch is a legendary money manager who took over Fidelity's Magellan Fund when it was an industry joke and turned it into the largest fund in the world. In the process he made a mockery of the notion that markets are unbeatable.

Then, at the peak of his game, he chucked it all to spend time with his family and began an equally successful career as a finance writer. In *One Up on Wall Street*, his first book, he sketched out his conception of the "amateur's advantage": "The amateur investor has a number of built-in advantages that, if exploited, should result in his or her outperforming the experts. . . . If you stay half-alert, you can pick the spectacular winners right from your place of business or out of the neighborhood shopping mall, and long before Wall Street discovers them."

He supported this assertion with dozens of examples of how his own alertness (and his family's enthusiasm for shopping) had made him and his clients rich. It's a great book, both because it's a lively read and because its author has a record that backs up his words.

And yet, reading Lynch is a little like listening to Michael Jordan explain how to dunk or Tiger Woods discuss putting. It's fascinating and certainly useful, but you just know that in addition to perfect technique, these guys have a combination of innate ability and hard-won experience that you can't match.

In Lynch's case, it's certainly true that the average person will turn up some interesting public companies in a lifetime of work and shopping, but probably not enough to build an investing career around. And when most investors find, say, a new restaurant they like, and take the next step of establishing that it's a public company based several states away, they're still left feeling somewhat isolated. Yes, the food is good, and yes, its stock seems to be reasonably priced, but they can't escape the sense that there is vastly more to be known and understood about this company before they can safely bet their savings on it. And if the company happens to be small and based far away, they're left with few sources of help, few sounding boards for their opinions.

Main Street, Not Wall Street shows investors how to get around this limitation by exploiting the one part of the amateur's advantage when there is information in abundance, available for the asking. Call it your "local advantage."

By plugging into the flow of local information, you can multiply your eyes and ears exponentially, virtually guaranteeing that when the next great company is born nearby, you will be there.

Three Things You Should Not Do

Yes, you do have an advantage over Wall Street when it comes to local companies. But you *should not* put all your money into such stocks. Your livelihood may depend on the health of the local economy, and certainly your home's value does, so it's imprudent to risk your whole nest egg on it as well. Investments in local companies should make up only a part of your portfolio, the part with which you try to beat the market.

Don't simply buy the stocks mentioned later in this book. They are illustrations, not recommendations. Most of them are "emerging," i.e., relatively small and as yet untested, and many of them will fail to live up to their early promise. In any event, their stories will be very different in a year or two.

And, finally, don't feel obligated to do everything recommended here. I've tried to lay out a range of possibilities for tapping into the local information stream. No one has the time to do it all, so you'll want to tailor a strategy to your temperament and circumstances.

On What Follows

This book is divided into three parts. The first part sets up the thesis of local advantage and explains it with statistics, anecdotes and profiles of the various players. The next addresses some general issues of investing and information management, as they apply to local companies. The third part is a listing—extensive but by no means comprehensive—of local sources for selected cities, along with the companies that went public in the year prior to June 1997.

Your diamonds are not in far distant mountains or in yonder seas; they are in your own back yard, if you but dig for them.
—Russell Conwell, *Acres of Diamonds*

Find smart people, because if you can do that, you can forget a lot of the other rules.
—Adam Smith's "Irregular Rules," *The Money Game*

1

YOU'RE HERE AND THEY'RE NOT

Pretty town, Bentonville, Arkansas. Nestled between the Ozark and Boston mountains, it's the kind of place where you might happily retire or settle down to raise a family. But for a decade or so beginning in 1970, Bentonville was also one of the easiest places in the world to be an extraordinarily successful investor.

In the 1960s, a young iconoclast named Sam Walton took a handful of Ben Franklin five-and-dimes and transformed them, by expanding selection and cutting prices, into Wal-Mart, the largest retail chain on the planet. Operating out of his Bentonville headquarters, "Sam" flew from town to town in his own Cessna, like a cross between the Music Man and Johnny Appleseed, sprinkling new stores wherever he touched down. In the process he made his early investors an amazing amount of money. A bet on his company at the time of its 1970 initial public offering returned eighteen hundred to one over the next twenty years. In other words, $1,000 became $1.8 million.

But the point of this tale isn't how many people were made rich by Wal-Mart, it's how many weren't.

When Walton took his company public in 1970, he had only eight hundred shareholders, most either "institutions or folks we knew," he wrote in his autobiography. Now, that might seem a reasonable number of shareholders for a relatively new and obscure store chain, but consider: In 1970 Walton had eighteen stores up and running on the outskirts of small towns in the region. And because huge discount stores were a novelty in 1970 rural America, the arrival of a Wal-Mart in Sikeston, Jonesboro or Claremore was news. It meant a whole new shopping experience for people used to tiny downtown boutiques. And it meant imminent extinction for many of those stores.

"Whenever we put a Wal-Mart store into a town, customers would just flock to us from the variety stores," Walton wrote. "When you move like we did from town to town in these mostly rural areas, word of mouth gets your message out to customers pretty quickly without much advertising."

Yet, of the dozens of small merchants who were driven out of business by those eighteen original Wal-Marts, and the thousands of people who shopped there or read about it in their local papers, very few asked themselves, "Is it a good investment?"

"It was always interesting to me," wrote Walton, "that, except for those folks who worked in our company, our stock got very little support early on from the folks right here in northwest Arkansas. . . . I think it must be human nature that when somebody homegrown gets on to something, the folks around them sometimes are the last to recognize it."

Therein lies a huge missed opportunity for individual investors, one that most of us are missing right now.

A Wal-Mart, of course, comes along once in a lifetime. But on a smaller scale, similar things are happening every day in every city. Companies are being born, new ideas are being tested, established firms are reinventing themselves. And much of it is taking place outside the view of the national media and the mainstream investment community, either because the companies in question are too small, or they've fallen out of favor, or they're in out-of-the way places.

But for the people nearby, there is information in abundance. Buildings are going up, workers are being hired, shoppers are admiring new stores. Local papers are covering it all; local brokerage houses are pushing the stocks. In short, you, the individual investor, are exposed to an extraordinary amount of early, and therefore useful, information simply by living where you do. Learn to seek it out systematically and then to interpret what you find, and your chances of investing successfully will go way up. But to understand just how big an advantage this is, it's first necessary to take a clear look at what Wall Street is actually selling you.

Wall Street: Myth and Reality

As it turns out, the single most important sentence in those glossy ads for mutual funds and stock brokerage services is the fine-print disclaimer that says "Past performance is no guarantee of future results."

Three decades of research have proven that for both large capitalization stocks and major mutual funds, yesterday's winner has a fifty-fifty chance of being tomorrow's loser, and vice versa. As a result, an individual investor cannot consistently beat the market by following the advice of the major brokerage houses or buying most of the large mutual funds.

An explanation for this can be found in the way the financial markets have changed in recent years. Financial institutions—pension funds, mutual funds and banks—accounted for less than one quarter of trading volume on the New York Stock Exchange in 1960. Today that number exceeds 80 percent, as individuals switch from stocks to mutual funds, and their pension funds—generally managed by large institutions—swell.

Currently, more than two hundred major institutional investors and another one thousand smaller ones are out there every day, sifting through the latest data, squeezing out inefficiencies. These billion-dollar pension and mutual funds need highly "liquid" investments. That is, they're limited to stocks large enough to accommodate millions of dollars coming and going without distorting the price.

The following table illustrates how concentrated institutional money and brokerage house attention has become in the top tier of stocks in a representative industry. Compare the first few public companies with the last few, and you'll see that large cap stocks are owned by far more institutions and covered by more brokerage houses. Smaller companies are, relatively speaking, overlooked.

Table 1.1
SIZE MATTERS
Retail Industry Stocks and the Institutions that Follow Them

Company	1996 sales ($ bil.)	Number of institutions that own the stock	Number of brokerage houses publishing earnings estimates
Sears Roebuck	35	555	25
Dayton Hudson	23	361	18
Federated Dept. Stores	15	330	21
May Dept. Stores	11	45	6
Dillard Dept. Stores	6	242	20
Harcourt General	3	217	3
Caldor	3	21	0
Ames	3	2	2
ShopKo	2	85	7
Neiman Marcus	2	78	8
Stein Mart	0.6	78	13
Bon-Ton Stores	0.5	20	2
Jacobson Stores	0.4	17	7
Zions Cooperative Merc.	0.3	0	0
50-Off Stores	0.2	7	0
SoloServe	0.1	0	0
Crowley Milner	0.1	6	1

Source: Ward's Business Directory, Financial Disclosure, First Call

The net result: Tens of thousands of analysts and money managers spend their days sifting through the publicly available data on the one thousand largest companies, looking for angles, piling in and out whenever something changes. In the process, they largely cancel each other out. It has become impossible for most of them to beat the market consistently because as a group they *are* the market.

And when you include the expenses associated with all this

activity—analyst and portfolio manager salaries, prime office space, computers, travel and trading costs—the average mutual fund actually underperforms most of the time.

Table 1.2
THE PROS VERSUS THE MARKET

Year	% of equity mutual funds outperforming the S&P 500
1980	45
1981	87
1982	66
1983	43
1984	24
1985	28
1986	25
1987	26
1988	47
1989	21
1990	38
1991	59
1992	58
1993	64
1994	23
1995	18
1996	24
1997 (first half)	5

Source: Lipper Analytical Services

But this hasn't changed the behavior—or the marketing strategies—of Wall Street's major players, for two reasons. First, when you're really, really smart, and you have the resources of a huge financial institution at your disposal, it's easy to believe that even in a supposedly efficient market, you'll be the one to succeed. Second, clients will pay hefty management fees only for a service that they believe adds value, i.e., advice that helps them beat a passive buy-and-hold strategy.

So the vast majority of analysts and money managers continue to put in long hours honing their analytical skills and looking for that one piece of information or that one insight that will give them an edge. And they continue to believe—and to tell the world—that this year they'll beat their markets.

Yet, as the table on the previous page illustrates, for most professional money managers this has become an exercise in futility. And this futility has become the dirty little secret of the investment world.

Charles Ellis's *Investment Policy: How to Win the Losers Game* is part of the core curriculum for the Chartered Financial Analyst program, the credential of choice for professional money managers. Here's his assessment:

> Unfortunately, however, security analysis does not appear to be a useful or profitable activity. The premise that professional investment managers can beat the market appears false, particularly for very large institutions that manage most of the assets of pensions funds. . . . In fact, given the cost of active management—fees, commissions, and so forth—most large institutional investors will, over the long term, underperform the overall market. Superior performance can be done and is done every year by some institutions, but it has not been done consistently over a long period of time by many.

Ellis's point is not that investment research is done ineptly. Just the opposite: So many people are doing it so well that—when it comes to the largest, most widely followed stocks—no one group of investors is likely to gain a consistent advantage. The market for large capitalization stocks is truly efficient.

Ellis concludes with some logical but still rather startling advice to money managers: Concentrate on schmoozing clients and minimize the time spent on picking stocks.

Market Timing: This Year's Guru

Related to, if not implicit in, the idea that professional stock pickers can beat the market is the idea that markets can be timed. That is, by watching this or that set of indicators, a sophisticated player can get in at the bottom and out at the top, avoiding both disaster and missed opportunity, and in the process outperforming a simple buy-and-hold strategy.

Capitalizing on this logical-sounding proposition, every major investment firm employs at least one high-profile "market strategist" to tell their clients whether now is the time to go from 60 percent equities and 40 percent bonds to 70 percent equities and 30 percent bonds.

But, for the most part, this, too, is wasted effort. For proof, you need to understand only one concept: Leverage. Today's crop of "derivatives," such as options and futures contracts (more about them in chapter 11), allows a speculator to control huge amounts of money with a small down payment. So anyone who can truly call the market's turns can, via market-based derivatives, make an ungodly amount of money in a short time. But a glance at the current list of the world's richest people yields not a single professional market guru. If they can't do it for themselves, they certainly can't do it for you.

The Impossible Opinion

I don't know this for a fact, but it wouldn't be surprising if every brokerage house training course devotes a day or so to "The Voice." This is the confident, knowing tone with which brokers and other financial advisers feed their clients insights into a given company's future.

Unfortunately, the company in question is usually a really big one.

For years, for instance, brokers sagely referred to IBM as "the best-managed big company in the world," while shoveling their clients' money into its stock. These days you're more likely to hear that honor bestowed on General Electric, often in concert with the opinion that its boss, Jack Welch, is a genius. AT&T, meanwhile, "owns the information superhighway." Microsoft is "king of the desktop."

The delivery is so smooth, and the sentiment so unassailable, that it's easy to overlook the fact that the statements themselves are virtually useless. Or, for the more cynical, fraudulent.

Your broker no more understands an entity as complex as General Electric—which is, after all, larger in some ways than many countries—than you know how the space shuttle works by watching it take off. To illustrate the point, let's take a look at exactly what GE does.

Table 1.3
GENERAL ELECTRIC'S BUSINESS LINES

Division	1995 revenues ($ bil.)	1995 operating profit ($ bil.)
Aircraft engines	6.1	1.2
Appliances	5.9	0.7
Broadcasting	3.9	0.7
Industrial products	10.2	1.5
Materials	6.6	1.5
Power generation	6.5	0.8
Technical products	4.4	0.8
Other	2.4	2.7
GE Capital	26.5	3.5
Eliminations	(2.5)	(2.4)
Total	70.0	11.0

Source: General Electric Corporation

GE operates in 100 countries. It has 250 manufacturing plants and employs 222,000 people. Of its 1995 revenue, 15 percent came from industrial products, including medical imaging equipment, motors and lighting systems, and 17 percent came from Europe. Another 37 percent came from its financial arm, which is essentially a big, powerful bank. Of its operating earnings, 11 percent were derived from aircraft engines. Its fastest growing division was broadcasting.

Its market capitalization as of April 1997 was around $200 billion, or slightly larger than the value of the entire Indian stock market.

Now consider how many smart people are sincerely trying to understand this company. According to First Call, a service that tracks such things, GE is currently covered by fourteen major brokerage houses. Its stock is owned by more than *two thousand* institutions, each of which presumably has an analyst assigned to follow it. And their composite opinion is what determines the price of its stock.

So, when someone tells you that GE's stock price is far enough out of whack to create a major buying opportunity, are they claiming insight into the demand for nuclear power plants in Europe? Or the future of broadcast networks vis-à-vis the Internet? How about the health of the aviation business?

It's a safe bet that they're clueless about most of the above. And yet, "That Jack Welch is a genius, he'll keep GE one step ahead of the competition." Well, maybe. But this is simply an acknowledgment of the fact that Welch has made good decisions in the past. It isn't analysis. And it's not something you should pay for.

Ditto for the Media

If most professional stock pickers underperform, it should come as no surprise that the torrent of advice flowing from the national financial media is also of dubious value. To test this for yourself, simply go to the library and dig out a back issue of a major magazine's "where to invest" issue, and check the results of their recommendations. In most cases, you'll find that they subsequently either matched or underperformed the market.

Here's one example from the dozens available: *Money* magazine's September 1991 issue included a table titled "20 great funds for a grand—or less." These five were the top picks in the growth category:

Table 1.4

	Average annual % return
Fund	*1/1/92–12/31/96*
Founders Frontier	16.52
Gabelli Growth	12.22
Janus	12.65
Nicholas	13.44
American Century: 20th Century Ultra	13.25
S&P 500	**15.19**

Sources: *Money* magazine and *Morningstar*

As you can see, four out of five funds came in well below the stodgy old S&P in the five years following their inclusion in the article. And these were the cream of the crop, chosen because of great track records, stability of top personnel and a whole host of other things that supposedly lead to superior performance.

Alas, all those brilliant analysts, portfolio managers and magazine editors, putting in seventy-hour work weeks with the latest analytical tools, essentially brought their clients and readers nothing. Looked at another way, everyone involved made money except you, the investor.

And Double Ditto for Investment Newsletters

The final refuge for people who don't trust the mainstream investment community is the shadowy world of investment newsletters. These typically revel in their challenge to the status quo and offer a unique set of insights that are guaranteed to keep you one step ahead of the pack.

But—you guessed it—as a group, newsletters have done even

worse than mutual funds. The *Hulbert Financial Digest*, for instance, tracks the performance of the major investment newsletters and publishes the results periodically. And as of January 1997, Hulbert calculated that only 27 out of 256 portfolios recommended by the major equity newsletters had outperformed the Wilshire 5000 over the past three years.

An Individual's Situation

For an individual investor, the point is clear, if a little eerie: When your broker calls and says it's time to get into IBM, she's simply guessing. When the next issue of *Business Week* presents the mutual funds that are sure things in the year ahead, it's just so much leisure reading. By and large, this is not useful information.

Which leaves you with two options. First, if you're among the vast majority who have neither the time nor the inclination to do their own investing, you're better off with index funds—that is, mutual funds that buy a broad spectrum of securities with the intention of simply matching a given market (see chapter 11). Such funds don't have to hire much high-priced talent, so they'll allow you to participate in the growth of a given market while demanding less in expenses. In the process, they'll beat the vast majority of actively managed funds.

If you're in the minority who have the time, interest and self-confidence to find and research your own investments, the only alternative is to find a niche, a little segment where you have access to information that has predictive value and is not yet widely disseminated.

That might be your field of expertise. If you're a salesman, you know who in your business has the hottest products, and so which stocks might do relatively well next year. If you're a parent, you know which toy companies are pushing kids' buttons.

But virtually all of us have one area of expertise: our communities. Unless you live on an Alaskan mountainside, there are public companies headquartered or doing significant business nearby. Most are small by national standards, and so don't draw the attention of more than a handful of institutional money managers. But they're familiar to their neighbors. You or those you know work for them, do business with them or, at a minimum, read about them in the morning paper. This is where you have an advantage, where you can, potentially, find investments that beat the market.

More Than You Think

A common reaction to the idea of investing locally is that a single city, region or state is simply too small an area to contain more than a handful of good investments.

Ten years ago, this would have been a legitimate concern. But no more. In the past few years, a combination of rising stock prices and the emergence of half a dozen or so new technologies has produced a boom in initial public offerings. Companies are springing up and selling stock to the public at a rate that's almost surreal.

In the following table, for instance, are the firms that went public in and around Denver, Phoenix and Columbus, Ohio, in the twelve months ending June 1997. The prior few years were similar, and the future looks even brighter.

These lists, along with the other hundred or so in the back

of this book, make the point fairly emphatically that emerging growth stocks aren't just a Silicon Valley thing anymore. They're everywhere, which means that many of them are right down your street.

Table 1.5
INITIAL PUBLIC OFFERINGS, JUNE 1996–JUNE 1997

Denver, Colorado
Coleman Natural Products (Beef products)
Imagematrix (Computer systems)
Jones Education Networks (Educational programming)
Jones International Networks (Radio and cable television)
Markwest Hydrocarbon (Natural gas)
Matrix Capital (Mortgage banking)
Metrogolf (Golf centers)
NAVIDEC (Internet services)
New Era of Networks (Software)
Osmotics (Skin-care products)
Premier Concepts (Retail stores)
Qwest Communications International (Fiber optics)
Racom Systems (Smart card systems)
Sportstrac (Sporting goods)
Startek (Business services)
Teletech Holdings (Customer-relations consulting)
Titanium Metals (Titanium sponge and mill products)
United Australasian Communications (Television services)
Vail Resorts (Ski resorts)
Wireless Broadcasting Systems (Wireless cable)

Phoenix, Arizona
Crager Industries (Custom vehicle wheels)
CSK Auto (Automotive parts retailer)
Eller Media Corp. (Outdoor advertising)
Schuff Steel (Steel construction services)
SkyMall (In-flight catalogs)

Styling Technologies (Personal-care products)
Ugly Duckling Corp. (Used cars)

Columbus, Ohio
Abercrombie & Fitch (Clothing stores)
Acorn Products (Lawn and garden tools)
Airnet Systems (Air transportation)
Bigmar (Drugs)
Karrington Health (Assisted-living services)
Nationwide Financial Services (Financial services)
Progenitor (Genetic engineering)

Source: IPO Data Systems

At this rate, it takes only a few years to produce a huge crop of young public companies, many of which are doing well, and most of which are utterly unknown to investors at large. The next table, for instance, lists *fifty* public companies headquartered in and around Dallas that grew by at least 38 percent in 1994.

Table 1.6
DALLAS'S EMERGING COMPANIES

Company	Business	1994 revenue growth rate %
Star Resources	Broadcasting	1,249
SA Holdings	Telecommunications	283
Polyphase	Computer networking	241
Heartland Wireless	Wireless cable TV	156
TGC Industries	Geophysical services	120
NRP	Marketing	110
Canmax	Software	108
Search Capital Group	Car receivables	98
Cyrix	Computers	97
CellStar	Cellular phones	88

Company	Business	1994 revenue growth rate %
USA Waste Services	Waste management	88
Arch Petroleum	Oil and gas	87
ProNet	Paging	87
Lomak Petroleum	Oil and gas	82
Coda Energy	Oil and gas	79
South West Property	Real estate	78
National Energy	Oil and gas	75
Encore Wire	Wire	66
NetWorth	Computer networking	63
Michaels Stores	Craft supplies	60
CompUSA	Computer stores	60
Box Energy	Oil and gas	60
D. R. Horton	Homebuilding	58
Optical Data Systems	Computer products	55
American Realty	Real estate	54
Fossil	Watches	54
Medical Resource	Medical equipment	54
Saber Software	Computer software	53
Wiser Oil	Oil and gas	52
MedicalControl	Medical-cost management	52
Ultrak	Closed-circuit television	50
Comstock Resources	Oil and gas	45
RF Monolithics	Radio frequency components	45
Affiliated Computer Services	Information processing	43
Hadson	Natural gas	42
Waste Recovery	Tire recycling	42
Westbridge Capital	Insurance	42
Integrated Security Systems	Security systems	41
DF&R Restaurants	Restaurant chain	41
The Great Train Store Co.	Train-themed merchandise	41
Renters Choice	Rent to own	40
Diagnostic Health Services	Medical services	39
Tecnol Medical Products	Medical products	39
Golden Triangle Royalty	Oil and gas	39
Business Records	Information services	38
Regent Technologies	Oil and gas	38
Bollinger Industries	Fitness products	38
DSC Communications	Switching systems	37

Company	Business	1994 revenue growth rate %
Bombay Co.	Furniture stores	37
InterVoice	Voice automation	37

Source: *Dallas Business Journal*

Note that while petroleum and computers are well represented here, they don't dominate the list. Dallas's menu of emerging growth contains everything from waste management to specialty retailing to medical technology. Just as important, you've never heard of most of them, and neither have most mainstream money managers.

Finally, to illustrate the connection between a company's early growth and its stock price, consider the following list of Cincinnati-area companies:

Table 1.7
CINCINNATI'S BIG WINNERS

Company	Low price since 1/1/90	Price 7/30/97	% change
Provident Bancorp	3.0	47.0	1,467
Omnicare	2.0	29.5	1,375
Comair Holdings	2.0	27.0	1,250
Pomeroy Computer Resources	3.0	32.5	908
Fifth Third Bancorp	6.5	61.5	846
LSI Industries	2.0	14.3	615
Star Banc	6.5	46.3	607
American Annuity Group	3.0	20.8	593
Cintas	13.0	66.0	408
Jacor Communications	9.0	43.0	377
Cincinnati Milacron	7.0	27.8	297
Cincinnati Financial	21.0	82.5	293

Source: *Business Courier*

Until recently, most of these companies were small enough to be overlooked by most major investing institutions. But they were well known at home. Newspapers covered them, local brokers recommended them, local people worked for and serviced them, et cetera. In short, years before the first Wall Street analyst walked into a research meeting and said, "Here's a little stock we might want to consider . . . ," thousands of people in and around Cincinnati knew something was going on. Those who followed up and acted have in some cases had their lives changed forever.

2

YOUR LOCAL BUSINESS JOURNAL: MORE GOOD IDEAS THAN *THE WALL STREET JOURNAL*

The desk isn't much to look at, with its pitted surface and scuffed edges. It fills a corner cubicle in a long, equally nondescript room in a building that's seen better decades. But this desk is special, because it's the delivery point for your local business journal's mail. Each morning, press releases, earnings reports and various other bits of news on the emerging companies of an entire city land here. An intern then pulls up a chair, cranks the volume on her Walkman, and starts slicing open envelopes. She routes some of what she finds to the appropriate reporters, some to editors. The rest she puts in a big loose-leaf binder for future reference.

By five o'clock, the day's raw material has been digested. Some of it has inspired feature stories, while some will be excerpted or reprinted verbatim. And the result will be a flow of investment ideas that's often far more useful than anything you'll see in *The Wall Street Journal*.

Don't misunderstand. I love *The Wall Street Journal*—and

Forbes, Fortune, Barron's, Business Week and *Investor's Business Daily.* All do a great job of covering capitalism's Big Picture. But as a source of emerging growth stocks, they have at least two near-fatal flaws: The size of their audience guarantees that when they discover something, it's seen by millions, minimizing its value for an individual reader, and their global reach means that most of their reporting involves companies headquartered far from wherever you are. So even if an idea in, say, *Investor's Business Daily's* superb "New America" section strikes you as a good one, you're left with few reliable sources of corroboration and follow-up.

With local media, precisely the opposite is true. When an earnings report or company profile appears in the local paper, it's seen by only a tiny fraction of the investment community, giving readers a piece of information that Wall Street may not have. And the companies covered by the local press are usually headquartered nearby, making the people who know them best your neighbors.

Now, your job is to figure out which parts of the local media do it best. An obvious, and generally pretty good, starting point is the business section of the daily newspaper. (See chapter 6 for a real-world example of how effective this can be.) But most towns now have an even better source of news on homegrown companies: a local business journal. Generally printed in a weekly tabloid format, though occasionally a glossy monthly, this is a publication that's dedicated completely to the business scene of one city or region. You may not be aware that your city has one, because they're usually marketed to companies and their executives rather than individuals. But in the business community, this is the bible of salespeople seeking leads, firms looking for customers and investors hoping for the next Wal-Mart.

The concept is relatively new; industry prototype *Crain's Chicago Business*, for example, has been around for less than two decades. And for much of that time it was thought that only the largest cities could support a separate business paper. In the mid-1980s, however, publishers began to notice an unsatisfied demand in smaller cities and regions. Local businesspeople wanted more insight into their customers and competitors than their general interest newspaper could supply. They also wanted a precise way to reach their customers with print ads.

Commerce abhors a vacuum, so the number of local business journals has exploded. Though no one keeps precise statistics, one industry organization put the total at more than three hundred in 1996, with the average journal's circulation running a little over ten thousand. And as publishing technology gets simpler, entrepreneurs are slicing and dicing their markets ever more precisely, creating journals for suburbs and smaller towns—and providing coverage for smaller and smaller companies.

"We follow the red herrings [the earliest document on soon-to-be-public companies] like you would not believe," says the editor of a city business journal. "A lot of the time we're the only source of public information on these guys." This near monopoly often lasts for years, until a company has grown big enough to attract out-of-town attention.

What to Look For in a Business Journal

Because the field is so new, many business journals' investment reporting is still uneven, with stock prices in one place, feature stories on public companies in another and other relevant sections, if they're included at all, scattered throughout the paper. As a result, much of the best stuff slips by readers who may not even know it's there, or, for that matter, what it means. It's therefore crucial to know what to look for, to figure out where your local business journal puts it and to be able to find it quickly at each reading. The following is an overview of what you'll want, with a brief explanation of why each is important. Later chapters will discuss how to interpret and act on what you find.

Feature stories on local public companies. Here's an excerpt from a *Nashville Business Journal* article on a restaurant chain that may be at a turning point. Because the company is relatively small, headquartered far from Silicon Valley and in a field that has nothing to do with the Internet, you won't see it profiled in *Barron's* or *Business Week*. It was, however, deemed big enough news locally to rate page one, above the fold.

On the Menu—Profitability: Higher Revenues, Earnings Now Served at O'Charley's
by Jamie Clary

In terms of a place to eat and a company to invest in, you might crave O'Charley's.

The Nashville company's stock price is holding at 14, from a 12-month low of 9½, while revenues for the first quarter

1997 ($56.7 million) finished 20 percent ahead of first quarter 1996 ($47.1 million). Net earnings for O'Charley's (NAS-DAQ: CHUX) first quarter were 29 percent higher at $2.3 million, or 27 cents per share, compared with $1.8 million, or 21 cents per share, in the same quarter in 1996.

Also during the first quarter, the company's same store sales were ahead of 1996's first quarter by 4.7 percent. During that time the company opened six new stores, including one in Lebanon, Tenn., to bring its total number of stores to 76. . . .

"Their comprehensive look at business lightened, brightened and increased the excitement in their restaurants," says Bob Derrington, senior vice president and a restaurant analyst for The Equitable.

The company did two other things in 1996 that made a significant difference this year, says Derrington. One was a set of menu improvements that highlighted the best items and added others such as combination platters and pasta dishes.

Costs in preparing pasta dishes typically are lower than other dishes.

Presently, J.C. Bradford rates the company a Strong Buy, just months after ranking it low among other restaurants in its 50 stocks that make up the J.C. Bradford restaurant index. Within the 50, O'Charley's finished third from the bottom in stock performance during the first eight months of 1996 while losing 22 percent of its value.

That was 1996, when the company was still dealing with a class-action discrimination lawsuit. Since then, the deadline to apply for part of the settlement has passed with only 25 percent of the potential plaintiffs responding, allowing the company to hold on to $2.3 million previously set aside for the settlement.

"1997 should be a better year for the company," states a February J.C. Bradford analysis. "Management's time is no longer being spent on the lawsuit, and earnings comparisons should not be affected by non-operating items as they were in 1996."

The author of that analysis, Barry M. Stouffer, says, "It looks like the company is back on track. And their stock is reasonably valued relative to the market, their growth rate and other companies with comparable growth rate."

As for the numbers that should be considered by investors, Derrington cites O'Charley's same store sales, traffic count and margin expansion. "Based on the trends, we believe the company will exceed expectations," he says.

This story gives the company's history, its current situation and the reasons for its possible comeback. And it quotes two local analysts who know the chain well, providing a reader with two (three, including the reporter) sources who can offer an informed opinion. For a Nashville resident, these guys are neighbors, and are therefore likely to return a call and answer a few well-chosen questions.

The stocks section. Most journals devote a page or two to a listing of local stocks. Some focus on which stocks are currently rising and falling most quickly, while others just list the stocks alphabetically and give some relevant data. The best stock sections also give an indication of each company's size by listing either market capitalization or sales. Combined with a growth rate for earnings, sales or stock prices, this allows you to identify quickly the small companies that are doing positive things.

Some other journals make readers work harder by listing the stocks without differentiating between blue chips and recent IPOs. Most will eventually fix this oversight, but in the meantime, a shortcut to identifying the relatively small companies is to note the exchange on which they trade. NASDAQ (also known as over-the-counter, or OTC) companies are generally smaller than NYSE or ASE firms.

Earnings reports. When a company's quarterly sales go from $3 million to $5 million, that's not national news, but it is a signal that something interesting is happening. Four of the five companies in the following example are both fast growing and small enough to have been overlooked by most money managers. Research them, and you'll be one of the few doing so.

Table 2.1
EARNINGS REPORTS

Rational Software Corporation (NASDAQ: RATL)

Quarter: March 31	1997	1996
Revenues:	$145.4 million	$104 million
Net income:	($42.9 million)	($3.6 million)
Earnings (loss) per share:	(98 cents)	(10 cents)

Healthcare Financial Partners, Inc. (NASDAQ: HCFP)

Quarter: March 31	1997	1996
Revenues:	$4.49 million	$2.28 million
Net income:	$1.21 million	$421,000
Earnings per share:	18 cents	7 cents

Industrial Training Corporation (NASDAQ: ITCC)

Quarter: March 31	1997	1996
Revenues:	$4.72 million	$3.72 million
Net income:	$456,000	$397,000
Earnings per share:	12 cents	11 cents

MCI (NASDAQ: MCIC)

Quarter: March 31	1997	1996
Revenues:	$4.9 billion	$4.5 billion
Net income:	$295 million	$295 million
Earnings per share:	42 cents	42 cents

Zygo Corporation (NASDAQ: ZIGO)

Quarter: March 31	1997	1996
Revenues:	$22.5 million	$15.2 million
Net income:	$3.7 million	$2.5 million
Earnings per share:	31 cents	22 cents

Source: *Washington Business Journal*

Insider transactions. In the hierarchy of information sources, a company's executives are at the pinnacle. They know how the new widget is selling, if the new plant is coming on line within budget and whether Microsoft is thinking of buying them out. The term "insider transaction" refers to what these guys are doing with their own shares of company stock. Generally speaking, if they're buying, that's good, and if they're selling, that's either neutral or bad.

Table 2.2
INSIDER TRANSACTIONS

Precision Castparts Corp.: Gamco Investors, Inc., bought 169,700 shares at $37.80 to $40.38. It now has 6 percent of shares outstanding.

Albertson's Inc.: John Carley, chairman, sold 120,000 shares at $38 to $38.88. He now has 543,900 shares.

Reebok International, Inc.: Robert Meers, executive vice president, bought 321 shares at $28.90. He now has 3,351 shares.

Schnitzer Steel Industries Inc.: Dori Schnitzer, director, sold 20,000 shares at $28.06.

TriQuint Semiconductor Inc.: Steve Sharp, chairman, sold 10,000 shares at $13.88. He now has 6,908 shares.

Kliener Perkins Culfield sold 204,037 shares at $22.13. It now has 375,000 shares.

Weyerhaeuser Co.: William Clapp, director, sold 115,000 shares at $43.88 to $46.13. He now has 326,621 shares.

Electro Scientific Industries Inc.: Leila Strain filed her intent to sell 3,000 shares, worth an estimated $67,500.

Source: *Business Journal* (Portland)

Stock profiles. Some journals devote half a page of each issue to a profile of a different local company. These aren't research reports, but they usually include some financial statistics and an overview of the company's business. The example that follows was excerpted from a stock profile in Portland's *Business Journal*. It shows a company with rising sales and a market cap of less than $100 million. Insiders own nearly half the stock, and the only two analysts covering it are at a local brokerage house.

Table 2.3
STOCK PROFILE

FEI, Inc.
NASDAQ: FEIC
7451 N.E. Evergreen Parkway, Hillsboro, OR 97214 (503) 640-7500

FEI Co. designs, manufactures and sells focused ion beam workstations and components based on field emission technology. Founded in 1971, the company went public in 1995.

Number of shares outstanding (as of March 31, 1995): 6,875,371
52-week price range (as of Oct. 31, 1995): $14.50–$10.
Close: $12.63
Approximate market value (as of Oct. 31, 1995): $86,835,936
Control by officers/directors as a group: 41.9%

PERFORMANCE

	1994	1993	1992
Net sales (000s)	22,281	$17,198	$12,919
Net income (loss) (000s)	($225)	$1,430	$411
Earnings (loss) share	($0.04)	$0.28	$0.08
Shareholder equity (000s)	$9,047	$9,231	$7,793
Return on equity	none	15.5%	5.3%

SIGNIFICANT STOCKHOLDERS (No. of shares, percent of class)
Capital Consultants, Inc., Portland, 715,910 (10.4%); State Farm Mutual
Automobile Insurance Co., 333,334 (4.8%)

ANALYSTS
David Duley, Black & Company, Inc. (503) 248-7525; Tom Mancino (415)
474-2096

General company announcements. This is probably the least read section of most business journals, but it's often the most interesting. Usually one page or less, it's devoted to a potpourri of local business events, including new contracts, acquisitions, bankruptcies, divestitures, et cetera.

But there's gold in there. For instance, a small company that gets a big new order might be on the verge of dramatic growth. The rest of the investment community won't notice until that order makes its way to sales or earnings. But there it is, right now, waiting for you.

Table 2.4
ANNOUNCEMENTS

MERGERS AND ACQUISITIONS

Metrocall Inc., an Alexandria-based messaging company, plans to purchase Dallas-based ProNet Inc., one of the biggest competitors, for $73.8 million.

Orbital Sciences Corp. of Dulles plans to purchase the satellite manufacturing and communications division of Rockville, Md.-based CTA Inc. for $37 million.

Star Technologies Inc., a Sterling-based software company, purchased Intrafed Inc., a Maryland-based software company, for $1.9 million plus 2.6 million shares of Star stock.

CONTRACTS

Branch & Associates, Inc., Roanoke: $8.9 million from Woodrow Wilson Middle School for renovations and additions.

BDM International Inc., McLean: $8.2 million over two and a half years from the state of Texas to rewrite the benefits systems for the Texas Teachers Retirement System.

K. F. Wilson Contractor Inc., Hampton: $15 million from the Naval Facilities Engineering Command for demolition work.

Versatility Inc., Fairfax: $3 million from British Telecommunications Plc for software installation.

STOCKS

Dollar Tree Stores Inc., a Norfolk-based chain of discount variety stores, plans to offer 3.5 million shares of common stock.

Jackson Hewitt Inc., a Virginia Beach-based tax-preparation service, sold 1.3 million new shares in a public offering for $23 million.

Source: *Virginia Business Magazine*

Coverage of private companies. Successful private companies are tomorrow's great growth stocks. But because they don't have to report their earnings—or much of anything else—they're largely anonymous to investors. The best local business journals make a real effort to keep up with the private side of their territories, giving their readers a chance to track these companies before they go public. Here's an excerpt from an article in the *Atlanta Business Chronicle* that goes on to list several companies likely to go public in coming years.

State Boasts Many Promising Young Companies
by Charles Davidson, Staff Writer

Georgia is home to many young technology companies that have a chance to become very successful. Following are descriptions of a few. The list is by no means a complete catalog, but rather a sampling of younger firms that bear watching during the next couple of years.

Telecom International Inc.
Who: Jack Acker is the CEO and founder. He was formerly group president of the network system group at Scientific-Atlanta, Inc. Other principals include Michael Ball, chief financial officer and former Scientific-Atlanta group vice president of finance, and Macy Summers, former director of technology for Scientific-Atlanta.
What: Telecom International designs and builds cellular and paging systems, and satellite-based telecommunications systems in emerging markets.
When: Founded in 1995
Where: Norcross
How much: First-year revenues were $7 million.
Paying the bills: The company has been financed internally and is employee owned.

The editorial staff. Some journals have reporters who specialize in local public companies. Other reporters might focus on a given industry, such as health care, real estate or finance. These specialties are often noted on the paper's masthead, like this one, which comes from the *Baltimore Business Journal:*

Terence O'Hara, ext. 113 *Editor*
Teresa Lindeman, ext.112 *Managing editor*
Cathy Gainor, ext. 111 *Associate editor*
Kevlin Haire, ext. 115 *Senior editor covering small business*
Charles Wolpoff, ext. 114 *Banking and financial services reporter*
Craig S. Ey, ext. 116 *Business and politics, technology and transportation*
Rob Kaiser, ext. 117 *Health care and international trade*
David Harrison, ext. 118 *Real estate, construction, accounting*
Donna DeMarco, ext. 119 *Retail, media, and marketing*
Heather Reese, ext. 121 *Researcher and manufacturing*
Antoinette Valentin, ext. 120 *Researcher and nonprofits*

The Book of Lists. This is the mother lode. Once a year, the best business journals publish compendiums of the local economy's vital statistics. These are usually large, thick volumes called the *Book of Lists,* or something similar. And they often contain a year's worth of research ideas. Besides the obvious "Fastest Growing Public Companies," many *Books of Lists* give the best and worst performing local stocks, the largest and fastest growing private companies and the leading companies' major local industries.

Variations on the Local Business Journal Theme

Then there are the publications that aren't local business journals but function the same way. Most states, for instance, have magazines that are mini-versions of *Forbes* or *Fortune*, often imitating the latter's standard features, such as the largest public companies, richest individuals, fastest growing firms, et cetera. And because most states are themselves a fairly limited beat, these magazines can focus on smaller companies at an earlier stage of life than the national media can.

Business North Carolina, for instance, does an annual roundup of the state's equities, and quotes frequently from local brokerage house analysts and money managers. The cover story of its January 1997 issue was "Star Stocks: Charting the future course of the brightest shares in our constellation of companies." This would, obviously, be a great source for someone living in Charlotte or Raleigh-Durham.

Virginia Business Magazine does many of the same things. And it pays me to write a column in which I use local sources of information to find local stocks. The magazine also has a Web site that allows readers to search a database of Virginia companies, including their financial histories, descriptions of their businesses, the names of analysts who cover them locally and links to their Web sites.

Then there are regional newsletters, a great example of which is *Marple's Business Newsletter*, which has been covering the Pacific Northwest for fifty years. It notes trends in the region's economy and passes on news of initial public offerings and the top picks of the region's brokerage house analysts and money managers. There are probably as many local investment ideas concentrated in its eight monthly pages as in any other publication in the region.

How to choose

Many cities now have several business journals. Your ideal solution to this embarrassment of riches is, obviously, not to choose but to subscribe to and read them all. If you're like most of us, though, you'll need to decide on one local business journal and stick with it. So, first identify the candidates by calling the chamber of commerce. They'll supply you with names and numbers. Then call the journals and ask for a few sample copies. Read them for how well they present the items listed in this chapter. Note whether they offer special services, such as a Web site with E-mail access to their reporters and links to the Web sites of local companies. Then choose one, subscribe and make it your one piece of essential reading.

3

YOUR LOCAL BROKER: BETTER CONNECTED THAN MERRILL LYNCH

If the prospect of turning a list of obscure local companies into an investment portfolio is a little intimidating (as it should be), you'll be happy to know that help is just a phone call away.

In most good-sized communities, regional and local brokerage houses make it their business to understand local companies better than anyone else. Ranging in size from giants like Dain Bosworth in Minneapolis and Robinson-Humphrey in Atlanta all the way down to boutiques with a few dozen brokers and one or two analysts, these off–Wall Street players are a diverse group. But most share at least a partial focus on the emerging companies of their regions.

Why? Because they know an advantage when they see one. "You can't compete on Wall Street's terms, so you have to find niches," explains the research director of a midwestern brokerage house. "There are very few things left that are proprietary in investing—investment banking, municipal bonds, local stocks. This is how we differentiate ourselves."

Another research director, this one at a small southern brokerage house, expands on the idea of local advantage:

There are only about 150 companies in the market area we
cover. We attend the annual meetings, we know the people
who work with a given company, we know their suppliers and
customers. If there's a meeting or press conference, we're
there. . . .

You can imagine how difficult it is for someone who works
in New York to fly down to visit the headquarters of one of
these companies. Certainly not impossible, but it shoots the
whole day. For us it's a lunch date. . . .

We watch [local companies'] fortunes ebb and flow, and we
get some sense of when a stock is a good buy and when it is
not. . . . I play tennis with a number of people locally who
work for [several nearby companies], and they'll tell me,
"Gee, our orders are picking up," or, "Business doesn't look
too good." That's not inside information. But when you're
talking to someone more frequently you're likely to be first
to hear when business conditions are improving. It alerts you
to check with the company and develop an idea of the overall
picture.

He says this is especially true with emerging companies: "We
really do have [small local companies] all to ourselves. We hear
about them first, we track them first, we see them change from
a concept to a company that's earning more and more each
year."

Adds yet another research director: "Often, we'll show a stock we like to one of our institutional clients, and they'll respond that their market cap minimum is $300 million. We say 'We'll call you when it doubles.' " But in the meantime, his retail (i.e., individual) clients are piling in.

To illustrate the local broker/small company connection, here's the July 15, 1997, recommended list of Van Kasper & Co., a San Francisco–based regional brokerage house. Note that the market cap of most of these companies is far below $1 billion. By way of comparison, Intel's is currently around $115 billion.

Table 3.1
SMALL IS BEAUTIFUL
A Regional Broker's Recommended List

Stock	*6/30/97* *Market cap ($ mil.)*
Activision	201
Amylin Pharmaceuticals	436
Benton Oil & Gas	435
Catalytica	231
ESS Technology	521
First Republic Bancorp	240
IMSI	46
Incyte Pharmaceuticals	703
Octel Communications	1,200
Protein Design Labs	515
Rainbow Technology	145
Raytel Medical	97
Rowan Companies	2,420
Tarrant Apparel	103
Zindart Limited	66

Source: Van Kasper & Co.

Unique Products

Focusing on local companies allows regional brokers to create
unique pieces of research, some of which are among the most
useful products in the investing world. Especially good are overviews of the local companies in a given industry, including the
up-and-comers that few outside the immediate area have heard
of. See table 3.2 for an excerpt (a very tiny one) from an overview of small Virginia banks, put together by Richmond-based
brokerage house Scott & Stringfellow.

This list makes two things immediately clear. First, even a
medium-sized state like Virginia contains a lot of publicly traded
banks. Second, most of these "community banks" are so tiny
that no one covers them. As the financial services industry con-
solidates, some of these lenders will be gobbled up. Some others
will do the gobbling. And because virtually no one is systematically monitoring the action down there, all kinds of inefficiencies will exist at any given time. The field is wide open, in other
words, for an enterprising individual investor.

As a starting point, a list like this one, compiled by investment
bankers and analysts who have both access to the numbers and
the expertise to sort through them, is a huge time-saver.

User Friendly

Regional and local brokerage houses have some other advantages that derive from the fact that they're relatively small and
headquartered nearby.

For one thing, it's easier for an investor to get into their
research loop. Merrill Lynch, the world's largest investment
firm, employs more than eleven thousand brokers and perhaps

Table 3.2
UNIQUE RESEARCH
Virginia Community Banks with Assets of $50 million to $100 million

Name of Bank	Total assets ($ mil.)	Total deposits ($ mil.)	% change (1990–91)	Loan loss reserve as % of total loans	Shares outstanding (000)	Year-end bid price ($)	Total market value ($000)	Return on average assets (%)
Salem Bank & Trust, N.A.	99.6	91.2	17.2	1.7	842	8.00	6,376	0.54
Bank of Floyd	99.0	88.2	4.2	2.3	116	95.50	11,114	0.57
First National Bank of Altavista	94.4	86.1	4.7	0.4	212	35.50	7,513	1.08
PNB Financial Corp.—Warrenton	93.1	84.3	2.3	3.3	252	45.00	11,340	0.17
Hallmark Bank & Trust—Springfield	91.9	76.9	16.4	2.4	1,729	9.00	15,561	−0.91
Independent Bank—Manassas	91.4	86.3	15.1	1.5	1,000	10.50	10,500	−0.38
F & M Bank Corp.—Timberville	88.2	75.8	3.6	1.0	399	38.50	15,378	1.61
Bank of Rockbridge—Raphine	84.9	77.6	16.8	1.1	578	18.00	10,395	1.48
Miners & Merchants B & T—Grundy	84.1	75.7	20.4	1.1	362	20.00	7,240	1.20
Virginia B & T Co.—Danville	82.3	73.2	3.4	1.0	238	45.00	10,692	1.57
South Boston Bank	80.6	74.6	13.6	0.4	220	75.00	16,493	0.83
Grayson National Bank—Independence	76.1	66.1	11.6	2.0	430	20.00	8,594	1.27
State Bank of the Alleghenies	74.5	68.1	15.4	0.9	570	13.00	7,140	1.40
Commonwealth Bankshares—Norfolk	73.6	65.9	−5.9	2.1	804	5.00	4,019	−0.29
United Financial Banking—Vienna	73.3	58.0	24.0	4.3	1,007	3.00	1,003	−1.42

Source: Scott & Stringfellow Investment Corp.

one hundred analysts. The brokers deal with retail customers. The analysts work primarily with big money managers, while simply mailing their research to brokers.

To protect analysts' sanity, brokers are seldom allowed access to them, and the average individual investor client has as much chance of talking to a Merrill analyst as he does of lunching with his congressman.

At a regional brokerage house, in contrast, the ratio of brokers to analysts might be less than twenty to one. Brokers and analysts tend to know one another, and speak fairly regularly. One of the sales pitches local brokerage houses use in hiring brokers is precisely this: access to analysts, and a chance to have some say in which companies get covered.

And because the client base of most small brokerage houses is weighted toward individual investors, their analysts are more open to speaking to a local group or investment club, or returning the call of a client with a legitimate question.

That means two things. First, you have a good chance of getting your questions answered substantively by an analyst, either via your broker or directly. Second, because local brokerage houses claim to consider their brokers and clients part of their research network, *you* can be a source of information for *them.* Unearth a small, promising local company and pass it on to your broker, and at a minimum you'll get additional information drawn from the broker's connections and his knowledge of the field. But there's also a good chance that your initiative will result in ongoing coverage by one of the brokerage house's analysts.

Problem resolution also has a different flavor when it's handled locally. As one of the research directors quoted above puts it, "The client can put his slender fingers around a local broker's neck. He can complain to the local manager, he can complain to the president of the company. He can go up into the operations department and get what he needs, without being told, 'Oh, we have to wait for something from New York.'"

In a society that's becoming increasingly anonymous, where toll-free numbers have replaced human contact, this alone might be worth the trouble of setting up a new brokerage relationship.

Choosing and Using

Getting the most out of a local broker depends on three things: finding the right brokerage house, choosing the right stockbroker and managing the relationship.

Finding the right brokerage house. The best way to determine which brokerage houses are primarily local is by looking at a copy of the local business journal's *Book of Lists*. There you'll probably find a page titled "Largest Area Brokerage Firms," or something similar.

The example that follows, taken from a much longer list published and compiled by the *Nashville Business Journal*, includes four brokerage houses based in that city, along with several other regionals that probably cover a fair number of Nashville stocks. Start with a list like this and you're virtually guaranteed to find a brokerage house that shares your focus on local companies.

Table 3.3
COVERING NASHVILLE

Name Address Phone	Agents registered to sell securities; total staff	Number of area locations; year founded in area	Location of headquarters
J.C. Bradford & Co. 330 Commerce St., 37201 615-748-9000	64 550	3 1927	Nashville
Equitable Securities Corp. 800 Nashville City Center, 37219; 615-780-9300	47 153	1 1930	Nashville
Wiley Brothers Inc. 201 Fourth Ave. N., 37219 615-255-6431	45 52	1 1945	Nashville
Edward D. Jones & Co. 125 N. Spring St., 37130 615-890-5122	31 76	31 1968	St. Louis
A. G. Edwards & Sons Inc. 230 Fourth Ave. N., Ste. 200, 37219; 615-244-4000	29 35	1 1970	St. Louis
Morgan Keegan & Co. 150 Fourth Ave. N., Ste. 1850, 37219; 615-255-0600	27 42	1 1981	Memphis
J.J.B. Hilliard, W.L. Lyons Inc. (800) 444-1854	24 36	5 1854	Louisville, KY
Heidtke & Co. Inc. Third National Bank Building, Ste. 1130, 37219; 615-254-0992	21 28	3 1983	Nashville

Source: *Nashville Business Journal*

Two other good sources of information are the *Securities Industry Yearbook* and *Standard & Poors Security Dealers of North America*, at least one of which is available at most libraries. Each gives city-by-city listings of brokers of all sizes and persuasions.

Here's the S&P entry for Black & Co., a Portland-based regional. Note "Specializing in Pacific Northwest Securities" in the description and the number of registered reps (twenty-one). A brokerage house of this size and orientation should have a handle on the emerging companies in and around Portland.

BLACK & COMPANY, INC.
■ (NASD) (N) (MSRB) (SIA) (SIPC) (1959)
One S.W. Columbia St. (97258)
Brokers, Participating Distributors & Dealers in
  Corporate & Municipal Securities; Specializing
  in Pacific Northwest Securities
Also Registered—AK; AZ; AR; CA; CO; DC;
  FL; GA; HI; ID; IL; KS; KY; LA; MD; MA;
  MI; MN; MS; MT; NV; NJ; NM; NY; NC;
  ND; OH; PA; RI; SC; SD; TN; TX; UT; VA;
  WA; WI
Officers—Lawrence S. Black, Chrm Emeritus;
  Ron Sauer, Pres; Dennis B. Reiter, Exec V-P &
  Chief Fin Officer; Laurie R. Miller, Exec V-P;
  Herbert D. Black, Sr V-P; Bill Frerichs
  (Institutional Sales), Jennifer B. Groves
  (Institutional Sales), Laura Black (Corporate
  Finance), Kathryn Mustonen (Cashiering Mgr),
  Tom Savinar (Sales), V-Ps
Compliance—Teri Duffy, Secy
Clear Thru—BankAmerica National Trust Co.
Correspondent—Pershing Div. of Donaldson,
  Lufkin & Jenrette Securities Corp.
Registered Reps—21
NASDAQ—BLAK
Employer's Ident. No.—93-0479581
Employees—57
Phone—503—248-9600; Trading-503—228-2868

Another source is the chamber of commerce. The person who answers the phone is unlikely to know anything about local brokerage houses, but someone there does. So, with a little persistence you'll be able to track down a few names this way.

And, as with anything else, the opinion of someone you trust is golden. If your friends have accounts with local brokers, their experiences could save you both time and trouble.

When you've narrowed the list to a handful, call and ask if they do indeed specialize in local companies and if they accept retail accounts. If they do, ask for the following:

- An information packet that includes the company's history, vital statistics and guiding philosophy. The ideal firm will have been around for a while (some trace their lineage to pre–Civil War days) and have a long history of working with local companies.
- Copies of their research, along with a listing of which companies they cover and a roster of their analysts by name and specialty. The research should be well organized and accessible. And the coverage list should include mostly small local and regional companies.

Here's an example from NatCity Investing, an Indianapolis firm that puts out concise, useful research on a variety of local companies. This report compresses a lot of financial information into two pages, along with an overview of what the company does as well as why the analyst thinks it's a good investment.

BRIGHTPOINT, INC.

(NASDAQ - NMS: CELL)

Research Update   *Jeffrey L. Davis, Securities Analyst*   March 29, 1996

BUY --- 12 MONTH TARGET $24

Recent Price	$17.25-$18.38
52-Week Range	$12.63-$20.63
Trailing 12-Month P/E	25.7x
Dividend / Current Yield	N/A
Market Value @ $18.25 Per Share	$209.9mm
Outstanding Common Shares (pro forma)	11.5mm
Float (pro forma)	8.6mm

IMPROVING MARGIN

December 31:	1997E	1996E	1995	1994	1993
Earnings / Share, $	1.40	1.07	0.80	0.51	0.37
Dividends / Share, $	N/A	N/A	N/A	N/A	N/A
Book Value, $	9.60	8.20	7.13	2.53	N/A
Price / Earnings, x	13.0	17.1	17.5	23.7	N/A
Price / Book Value, %	190	222	196	478	N/A

COMPANY PROFILE

Brightpoint, Inc. (CELL), a worldwide distributor of wireless communication equipment and related products, commenced operations in 1989 as Wholesale Cellular USA, Inc. The predecessor company conducted its initial public offering of 2,300,000 shares @ $5.00 in April 1994. CELL's September 1995 five-for-four stock dividend preceded an October equity offering of 1,927,500 shares @ $19.00 (net proceeds of $33.9mm). This funding together with the January expansion of its bank credit line from $30mm to $50mm provides CELL with the developmental and working capital necessary for greater market penetration. Accordingly, CELL has recently announced a stock acquisition, a joint venture and a service contract facilitating mass market distribution of wireless products throughout the U.S.

HIGHLIGHTS

♦ Just this week, CELL announced an end-user product **fulfillment services contract with U. S. Communications, Inc.** (USCM). Such contracts are integral in CELL's strategic effort to increase value-added servicing and thereby enhance margin. Relative to this contract, CELL will repackage all product associated with USCM's retail sales efforts conducted through mass merchandisers and direct marketers. USCM currently has merchandising agreements with such well-known national retailers as Target, Lowe's, CompUSA, Osco Drug, Meijer, Kmart, OfficeMax, Service Merchandise and Montgomery Wards Electric Avenues as well as such direct marketers as QVC, Fingerhut and Spiegel. By October 1, USCM will have established approximately 5,500 in-store self-service kiosks featuring its "Cellular on the Go" kit — a cellular phone and an 800 number for remote activation processing from one's home or office. CELL's fulfillment effort, for example, will insure the necessary pre-programmed carrier distinctions between "Cellular to Go" sold at a east coast Target location vs. a midwest Target store. USCM has agreements with more than 60 cellular carriers across the United States.

First year revenues to CELL are estimated at $8mm, while the earnings contribution could approach $750m. Presently estimated at 34mm, the U.S. cellular subscriber base is projected to increase to 75mm within 5 years and 100mm by the year 2003. This implies mass market penetration, which in addition to product availability will also be encouraged by 1) lower airtime costs — USCM will take its marketing leverage to the major carriers, negotiating for airtime rates less than $20 per month, 2) growth of personal communications system (PCS) technology and 3) increased use of paging devices.

♦ CELL continues to pursue a May "pooling of interest" **acquisition of Allied Communications** as was announced January 23 — 2.5mm shares to be issued. Allied's 1995 sales of approximately $150mm reflect a strong relationship with cellular manufacturers Ericsson, Mitsubishi and OKI as well as a successful marketing effort in both the U.S. (northeast and mid-Atlantic) and Latin America / Puerto Rico (approximately one-third of sales). The combined entity will also benefit from an improved value-added focus, e.g., fulfillment, continued emphasis on low overhead and U.S. agent penetration.

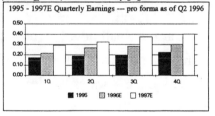

1995 - 1997E Quarterly Earnings — pro forma as of Q2 1996

Choosing the right broker. Once you've found a brokerage house with the requisite local focus and good research, you'll want a broker who shares your point of view.

The importance of this step can't be overstated, because even at local brokerage houses, brokers come in every size, shape and preference. Some are kids just out of school with little investment expertise and few local contacts. Some are highly professional, but more focused on mainstream investing and financial planning. But a few are exactly what you're looking for.

Early in the process of researching for this book, I had the good fortune to speak at length with John Peyton, a broker with Dain Bosworth in Minneapolis who specializes in finding small local stocks before his firm's research staff has noticed them. With the prospect of only a brief profile in my low-circulation, not-yet-very-professional newsletter, Peyton spent several hours telling me what he does and which companies he likes. The transcript of our talk goes on for several pages, but here are some excerpts to give you an idea of what you're seeking:

On his own background: "I'm fifty-one, a graduate of the University of Minnesota. I've been in Minneapolis my whole life other than a one-year stint at Colorado College and a five-month tour in the Coast Guard Reserve. I've been at Dain Bosworth for almost twenty-six years. . . . Minneapolis is a big town but also a small one. I've been here my whole life, and if I don't know someone, my friends do."

His main sources of ideas:

- The golf course.
- Dain Bosworth's investment bankers: "They know the people running local companies. There are restrictions on what [investment bankers] can talk about, but they can answer ques-

tions like 'Who's your favorite company?' and 'Do you like the guys running this company?' "

A typical course of research: "I might hear through a contact that a new company is doing something interesting. Then I'll start calling my other contacts, people in the company's field. I'll ask abut the products, and what kind of a reputation management has. Then I'll visit the company, meet management in person."

How he found two past winners:

- "I was playing golf in Naples, Florida, with a guy from GTE and he said, 'You guys have a company up there in Minnesota that has a helluva software product.' "
- After hearing good things about a local maker of burglar alarms, "I called a guy who used to caddy for me and now works in Honeywell's [Minneapolis] security division. He said their products are first-rate."

There's a lot more, including the standard discussion of earnings and growth rates, but you get the idea. Peyton's research methods rely on a lifetime of local connections and an enthusiasm for making new ones. It's light-years beyond "That Jack Welch, he's a real genius," and it's the kind of expertise and attitude you want in a local broker.

Once you've found a brokerage house that seems right, call it and ask for the names of several veteran brokers—people who have been at it for a while and presumably know the local scene well. Call them (noting how long it takes them to get back to you) and explain that you want to build a core portfolio of local emerging growth stocks. Ask them the following questions:

- *Do you specialize in local companies?* The answer should be an enthusiastic, long-winded yes.
- *Can you tell me about a local company you discovered, and document what happened?* A broker who has been working with local companies for any length of time will have plenty of examples at his fingertips.
- *Is it possible for a client to speak to your analysts?* The right answer is a qualified yes. A good local broker will act as a screen to protect analysts from uninformed questions. But the broker himself should have easy access to his firm's analysts and be able to get answers to your questions quickly.

Managing the relationship. Once you've chosen a brokerage house and settled on a broker, you're ready to begin a collaboration. Do not view this person as an order taker, but as a partner. You want his ideas on local companies. But you also want a sounding board for your own ideas. When you discover a company on your own, one of the first calls you should make is to your broker. In many cases he'll be aware of the company, or the entrepreneur who founded it. Or he'll know the competition and will have tips on what to look for and how to define success.

If the company is indeed promising, he'll also bring it to the attention of the research staff and perhaps get it added to the coverage list, making your job infinitely easier.

4

Your Friends: Better Informed Than Louis Rukeyser

Think fast: Your brother-in-law walks into the room, slumps into the easy chair and moans, "I can't take it anymore. This job is killing me." Do you:

A. Nod sympathetically and say, "Why don't I fix you one of those rum drinks you like so much?"
B. Leave the room with a terse "Sorry, I already hear too much of this from my side of the family."
C. Ask in a reassuring voice, "Why are you so busy? Tell me about your company. . . ."
D. A, then C.

If you answered either C or D, you're getting it. Because if your brother-in-law works for a public company and the job is stressful because of the firm's success rather than his incompetence, he's offering you a potentially valuable piece of intelligence. Same thing if his company is getting creamed by a local competitor or is straining to fill an order from a growing local firm. All are things that may not be widely known. And all might point to an undervalued local stock.

Now consider that you have dozens, maybe hundreds, of friends, family, co-workers, customers, competitors and associates, many with access to similar bits of useful data, and you'll begin to appreciate just how much information is potentially available from people you don't normally think of as investment advisers.

Unlike local brokers and business journals, these people don't get paid for collecting information and passing it on to you, so finding them and getting them to talk is a little trickier. But they can be found and are often willing to talk if approached in the right way.

Your Customers

In most ways it was a typical sales call. Scott Bauman, a Roanoke, Virginia, entrepreneur, had visited a new local company called Optical Cable and was pushing hard to make it a steady customer for his firm's factory supplies.

"As I was leaving," he recalls, "I asked [an Optical Cable co-founder] what else I could do for them. He said, 'Well, you could invest in us.'

"I had a couple of bucks in my pocket at the time," says Bauman. So he researched the company and found that it had a growing niche in fiber optics and a management team with plenty of experience. Impressed—and of course interested in anything that might cement a new business relationship—he took a flier and invested fifteen thousand dollars.

Optical Cable did well early on, just as Bauman expected, and three years later it bought him out for better than triple his original stake.

Meanwhile, it kept buying his products. "I watched its growth just explode," he says. "I was chomping at the bit to get back in. Whenever I saw them I'd ask when they were going public." When the IPO finally came, Optical Cable gave its former investors first crack. And despite advice from his broker and others to steer clear of the risky stock, "I jumped on it," he says, at (a split-adjusted) $2.50.

Then things got positively surreal. Optical Cable, hitherto unknown, caught the eye of enough out-of-town money to send its stock above thirty dollars within the year. Bauman bailed out along the way for a 900 percent gain. When the dust had settled, he found that he'd made more money by investing in his customer than by working with it.

The lesson? Your dealings with your customers put you in a unique position to judge who is succeeding and who is not. And, by extension, who is a timely investment. They're sending you countless signals—by building new factories, opening new stores, hiring new management, introducing new products, buying more equipment—much of which you'll notice long before Wall Street does.

Looked at another way, one or two of your customers, right this minute, might be worth more as investments than as business relationships. If you can identify them, you can raise your pay scale dramatically. So, if you work in sales, note which products are moving, and who is introducing them. When a customer doubles its order rate, don't just stock up on whatever they're buying. Find out why this is happening. If you buy a piece of equipment that works beautifully, that pays for itself in no time, that is supported by a crack staff or for whatever other reason is a must-have, don't just budget in several more purchases; find out who sells it and get to know them.

A final benefit of treating your customers as potential investments is that it forces you to understand them better than you might otherwise. This can't help but make you better at your job.

Your Competitors

In the annals of great missed opportunities, IBM's failure to buy part of Microsoft surely ranks near the top. It was the early 1980s, and the two were not yet bitter enemies, but rather uneasy collaborators/competitors on personal-computer software. Microsoft, hoping to solidify the relationship, repeatedly offered part of itself to Big Blue.

But IBM passed, and Microsoft went on to eat IBM's PC lunch, making its investors a fortune in the process. Had Big Blue simply bought, say, 20 percent of Microsoft early on, it would have earned more from this investment than from all the computers it sold in the subsequent decade. And today, most 1980s-vintage IBM execs are long gone, while Microsoft founder Bill Gates is the richest man in the world.

Now, you aren't IBM, thank heaven, but if you're in business, you have competitors who are rising and falling. Perhaps you cooperate on one level and compete on another; perhaps you spend your days plotting their destruction. Whatever the relationship, you are in a unique position to know how they're doing. And if they're succeeding despite your best efforts, you'll see it long before Wall Street.

Obviously, there are one or two ethical dilemmas involved in investing in a competitor, which I'll leave for you to sort through. But at certain times and under certain circumstances, your highest income might indeed come from swallowing your pride and buying a piece of the company that just stole your biggest client, or introduced a product that outperforms your best model. If anyone points to this as a conflict of interest, simply call it an attempt at industrial espionage and tell him to mind his own business.

Your Employer

I write a column on local investing for *Virginia Business Magazine* here in Richmond. The magazine, in turn, is owned by a local conglomerate called Media General. In the early 1990s Media General owned a small New Jersey newspaper chain that had fallen on hard times during the 1990 recession. Playing it safe, Media General wrote off the full purchase price of the chain, reducing its value to zero on the balance sheet.

A few years later, the market turned up, and Media General began negotiating the sale of this chain. Rumors were swirling within the *Virginia Business* offices that the offers were higher than expected, but nothing had appeared in the press or local brokerage house reports. Curious, I called an acquaintance on the company's corporate staff and asked about the rumors.

"Yeah," he replied, "it's worth more than we thought—the bids are around forty million dollars." That was serious money in this context, representing a windfall of maybe three dollars a share on a stock that was at the time around twenty dollars. Why, I asked my acquaintance, hadn't this appeared in the press? "No one has asked," he replied.

The deal was consummated, the profit recorded, and Media General's stock rose by about 50 percent over the next year, in part, I suspect, because the capital gain implied that more such undervalued assets might be hidden away in that company's complex balance sheet.

This was not a big deal in the grand scheme of things, but it does illustrate the kinds of information that are available inside a company long before the rest of the world catches on.

If you work for a public company, you therefore find yourself in a situation that's both interesting and difficult. If you're paying attention, you're exposed to an extraordinary amount of useful information. And you have the opportunity to buy your company's stock, either on the open market or via internal stock ownership plans. This is a life-changing relationship for some people; it's common, for example, for employees of successful emerging companies to make more money from their stock than from their paychecks. But it's also common for employees to lose everything, their jobs and their nest eggs, when their company fails.

So it pays to apply basic security analysis to your employer, but even more carefully than with an unrelated company.

Some tips: Start paying attention to your company's strategic planning. Are they buying other firms, building factories, expanding into new lines of business? Note what insiders are doing with their stock; this may be available within the company, and is reported by some information services and generally in the local business journal.

And identify the best sources of inside information. The investor relations department employs people whose job it is to answer investors' questions, making them good sources for general data. But people in Finance or Strategic Planning often have a better handle on the future. So be nice to these folks—they may be just as important to your earning power as your boss is.

Once you have a handle on your company's prospects, adjust your investing accordingly. Does a major turning point appear imminent, the kind that will send the stock much higher in a short time? If the answer is yes, buying as much stock as possible now makes sense. Or are you seeing solid, long-term thinking that makes you comfortable with adding to your stake gradually?

And because so much is riding on your company's success, pay special attention to signs of trouble. These can range from narrowing margins on a key product or footnotes in the 10-Q report noting money borrowed from or loaned to insiders all the way over to closed doors and long faces on executive row.

Another benefit of analyzing your employer is that it sensitizes you to opportunities and risks affecting your job. For instance, an expansion into a new product line or geographic area creates all kinds of new, high-visibility slots, while the acquisition of a competitor might mean the elimination of some redundant positions, including yours. Both are signals to update the résumé and start planning your next move.

One last thing: Some of what you hear is likely to fall into the "material, nonpublic" category, which makes its use illegal.

So you'll want to pay careful attention to chapter 11, where the concept of insider trading is defined.

Your Favorite Stores

All-you-can-eat restaurants aren't for everyone. But every once in a while, the urge comes over some of us to abandon nutritional good sense (and write off the rest of the day) and just pig out. A few years back I talked April into visiting a restaurant called Old Country Buffet, whose ads made it sound ideal for this kind of debauchery. And it was. It featured an entire serving table dedicated to fried chicken, another containing only desserts, and all of it was mine, mine, mine. I was happy, but, intriguingly, so was my wife, once she discovered the table of salad fixings and fresh fruit.

That Old Country Buffet worked for both of us was impressive. And based on the size of the crowd that day, it appeared to work for others as well. An hour or so later, as we waddled toward the door, I wondered aloud whether this place was owned by a public company, and April responded that we should look into it. Neither of us did, though, and the subject was forgotten until maybe a year later, when I noticed a story on how hot specialty-restaurant chains had become. Among the companies mentioned was Buffets, Inc., owner of the Old Country Buffet chain. Its stock had tripled in the year following our pig-out.

I've been bothered by this lapse ever since. I'd eaten there, loved the food, seen that it appealed to customers as dissimilar as me and April, noted that it was crowded, even spoken the words "I wonder if these guys are public?" And then I failed to follow up, and blew a chance to finance our son's college education.

Very annoying. And very common. This is something the average person does many times in the course of a normal life. We shop at a new store, eat at a new restaurant, buy a new product. We're impressed enough to go back and give them more of our money. But, like the early Wal-Mart shoppers in chapter 1, we fail to make the conceptual leap from "nice store" to "good investment?."

The solution, however, is simple. Just develop the habit of discovering who owns your next big find. Ask the waitress/sales clerk/cashier whether it's a public company. Then ask where it's headquartered. Then call for information.

Over the course of a consuming lifetime, this kind of attention will turn up a fair number of Buffets, Inc., and maybe even a Wal-Mart or two.

Simple Questions

One thing you may have noticed so far is a lack of technical jargon in the questions that local investors ask. This point deserves emphasis: It's not necessary to be a detective or a hypnotist—or an accountant—to find out what the people around you know about nearby companies. By simply working a few casual questions into your conversation you can find out quite a bit, without annoying others or putting them on the spot.

Don Bishop, for example, is a loan officer with a small New England bank. Each year he participates in the stock-picking contest run by the *Worcester Business Journal*. And between 1990 and 1995 he was consistently one of the top finishers, generating a *documented* return of better than 100 percent annually.

How? "It's not rocket science," he says. When he meets with

clients, he simply makes it a point to ask where they work and how they like it. "That's where most of my big winners came from."

They were companies he'd never heard of (even though he's a banker and they were headquartered nearby), but when his clients said positive things about them, he noted their names and followed up.

All of the above are good sources of information on local companies. But the best source of all is another dedicated local investor. Here are three organizations that make it easy to find your counterparts:

Investment Clubs

When Lindsey Barron arrived for her first day of teaching at Fallon Park Elementary School in Roanoke, Virginia, her new co-workers were cordial. They asked about her background, her family, her husband's job, et cetera. But when she mentioned that her husband worked for a local company called Optical Cable, the questions turned unusual.

"Public or private?" asked one teacher. "Does he think it's a good company?" asked another.

It turned out that several of the teachers had recently formed an investment club. They'd read *The Beardstown Ladies' Common Sense Investment Guide*, a book about sixteen Illinois women whose club regularly beats the market. As a result, they were beginning to view the world through green-tinted glasses.

Barron responded that to her knowledge Optical Cable was a

private company, and yes, her husband was enthusiastic about its future. There the matter rested until later that year, when the local newspaper carried an article about Optical Cable's plan to sell stock to the public.

Instead of passing by this tidbit without a second glance, the teachers, now familiar with the name and recalling their new co-worker's husband's enthusiasm, called the company for more information. They found a small, fast-growing maker of fiber-optic cable, the asphalt of the information superhighway. It was headquartered only a few miles away, but was so new that even in a town as small as Roanoke, few had heard of it.

Intrigued, the teachers divided up the task of learning more. A few went to the library and read up on the industry, coming away impressed with the potential of fiber optics in education, communications and entertainment.

Several others called the company and asked if they could visit the plant. Because they were both neighbors and potential investors, the company greeted them warmly, giving them a guided tour and even a brief, pleasant meeting with the founder. The teachers liked the clean, efficient-looking factory, judged sensible Optical Cable's plan to double its manufacturing capacity, and were charmed by the openness of management.

So, when the IPO price was set at a modest (adjusted for subsequent splits) $2.50 a share, "We got our money together and FedExed it in," says a club member. "Most of us had never done anything like [buying into an IPO] before."

One teacher bought 200 shares for herself and 100 for her daughter. Another bought 400. Cumulatively they bought around 2,000 shares. Then they looked on in amazement as Optical Cable became one of the year's remarkable IPOs. In the space of a few months, it ran to over $30 before settling into a $12 to $15 trading range. Their $5,000 investment had ballooned to $25,000.

These days, lunch breaks at Fallon Park have taken on an added dimension, with the market as much a topic of conversation as troublesome kids and clueless parents. "We were in the right place at the right time," concludes a club member. "The Beardstown Ladies had better watch out."

Several things about this story are noteworthy. First, the teachers used local sources of information from beginning to end, including a co-worker's husband's take on his employer, an article in the town paper and a tour of a local company. Equally important, this was a group effort, in which one person had a family member employed with the company, another asked about it and remembered the answer and still others did significant research and legwork. Finally, it was fun, a shared experience that ended well and added a new dimension—and a nice chunk of cash—to the lives of all involved. The teachers were, in short, able to accomplish something by working together that most of them would have been unable or unwilling to do alone.

Therein lies the power of investment clubs—groups of people, often neighbors or co-workers, who pool their ideas and learn about investing together. They make friends, some of them make money and they all learn a lot.

But most important for the purposes of this book, investment clubs are tailor-made for finding and analyzing local companies.

A little history. The first investment club is thought to have been formed in 1898, when a Texas railroad paymaster named A. L. Brooks became tired of seeing his co-workers frittering away their paychecks. Their numbers grew steadily over the next ninety years, as each generation of Americans came to the twin conclusions that they'd better learn to manage their money or they'd never get that Winnebago, and that the learning process is less painful if it's shared with a few like-minded friends.

But the concept really took off in 1994, with the publication of the Beardstown ladies' best-seller. In the three years following the book's release, the number of registered clubs shot up from 9,000 to more than 25,000. At year end 1996, the National Association of Investors Corporation (NAIC), the leading sponsor of investment clubs, had 350,000 members, about two thirds of whom belonged to a club. Together they invested about $12 million a month.

But, as with most other financial tools, an investment club doesn't improve your chances of beating the market if you're focusing on far-off large-cap stocks. Ten people in Tucson are no more likely to understand GE or Merck than one person alone with a copy of *Value Line*.

Yet that's exactly what most investment clubs attempt to do. According to the NAIC, the most commonly held stocks in investment club portfolios are, well, the most commonly held stocks: GE, Coca-Cola, Wal-Mart, McDonald's, Motorola. These are superb companies, but with them more eyes do not equal greater understanding. In fact, members of an investment club can get exactly the same result with less hassle (though also, admittedly, less fun) by buying a large-cap index fund.

But with local companies, an investment club is a different, more interesting animal. It might be, in fact, the best way to cover all the local bases. There's a lot involved in starting and running an investment club that is not covered in this chapter, including designing a charter, deciding who keeps the records and who writes the checks, and where and when to meet. The NAIC offers copious how-to material on these generic aspects of investment clubbing. Instead, let's look at ways to turn an investment club into your own private local-company research department.

If you'd like to join an existing club, look for one that already focuses on local companies. Some, though by no means most, do. If that's not possible consider starting one from scratch. Some tips:

Members. Choose members, first and foremost, because you enjoy their company. This is a long-term relationship that will require communication, negotiation and consensus. So making it work is much easier if you get along on a personal level.

But beyond the basic requirement of a reasonable personality, go for variety in occupation, educational background and life history. This way, you get as many viewpoints, and as many social and work connections, as possible.

Planning the first meeting. Make it clear to everyone you invite that the first meeting will be for discussion only, and that showing up does not imply a commitment to join.

Before the meeting, several members should read some how-to material and familiarize themselves with the nuts and bolts of running a club. Be prepared to answer questions, and bring along as much background material as possible for the inevitable questions you can't answer.

Setting the investment strategy. "Very few clubs have been successful in using a short-term, speculative approach to investing; those which have amassed large sums over the years have had a long-term outlook," says one of the NAIC's newsletters.

This is especially true with local emerging companies, because you're looking for a handful of long-term winners that start small and over a period of years wax big and successful. If history is any guide, this will be accompanied by some truly hair-raising twists and turns. To profit from the upswings that follow the corrections, you'll have to be prepared to sit tight for a long, long time. It's therefore crucial that the club's basic strategy— long-term investing in local companies—be understood and accepted by all members.

Talk this over, and ask for a show of hands of those who would like to continue. Then, once the team is in place, begin the process of connecting it to the local information flow.

Choose a local broker. The club will probably trade through only one account, and this is your single most important link to the universe of local companies. So choose a local broker for your club just as you would for yourself: Both the broker and his firm should be focused on local companies. The firm's research should be coherent and logical and the result of personal contact between analyst and company. And the broker should be willing to work with your club, attending and/or addressing your meetings occasionally.

Make it clear to the brokers you interview that this is a relationship with considerable long-term potential. For example, if ten of you put in $50 a month, that's a total of $500 a month, or $6,000 a year. Not a big deal at first, but over, say, a decade, it becomes real money. Most brokers will jump at the chance to nurture such a future income stream.

But don't stop with just one local broker. Because the club account is separate from members' personal accounts, individual members can open accounts with other brokers and/or brokerage houses that focus on local stocks. This multiplies the number of non–club members who are out there working for you.

Subscribe to several local business journals or other similar publications. Then assign a member to read each thoroughly and bring what they find to the club. Or pass each issue around to different members.

In this way you blanket the local media, ensuring your shot at the small stories that will later blossom into headlines.

Start a contact file. Have everyone sit down and think about people they know who might have information on local companies. Think in broad terms, including people who supply products like building materials, who offer services like computer consulting, who work for temporary staffing companies. Over time, note whom you meet and add them to the file.

Expect to call on these people when their expertise is needed. Often a simple "Do you know anything about XYZ Corp.?" will yield a surprisingly valuable answer.

Divide up the work. Once you start noticing interesting companies, you'll need to divide up the research work. One strategy is to assign different tasks to different members.

One member might research a given company's industry, noting growth trends, profiling the competition and establishing who covers the companies and how the market values them. This might be done via articles from the national press, local brokerage house research reports, *Value Line, S&P* or whatever else is available at the local library. It can also include questions submitted to a local brokerage house analyst who covers the industry.

Another member could do some basic security analysis on the company, including trends in earnings and sales and the solidity of the balance sheet. In the process, she may want to call the company, and possibly visit it. If one club member is especially Internet literate, she may want the job of researching companies on-line. See chapter 9 for more on how this works.

Another approach is to assign a given company to each member. Have them attend the annual meetings, get on their mailing lists, call and form a relationship with their investor relations staffs. They should also research the competition, including who does what in the field, how successful they are and how they relate to the local company.

Each person should be prepared to make a brief presentation covering the assigned company, its business, its growth prospects and an assessment of relevant local sources. They may also want to type up short reports that summarize their findings. See chapter 10 for some tools to make report generation easy. And don't limit your buying to the club. Early on, especially, your club's resources will be limited. But you can buy the stocks your club discovers for your own account. In short, think of your investment club as your own private research department.

Here's a real-world example that I turned up while researching a company called MedCath. While checking to see if the company had a Web site, I entered its name in a search engine and came up with, among many other things, the CCDS Investment Club in Charlotte, North Carolina. CCDS had posted its portfolio on its Web site, and had recently bought into MedCath, which is headquartered nearby. I noticed that several of the club's other stocks were based in the state and E-mailed them a question about their philosophy. Here's their response:

> In reference to your question about focusing on locally owned companies, and how we went about choosing them, our board of directors asked each club member to think of one or two stocks that they had been following lately, or had some kind of interest in. We then took this master list and sat down and debated the pros and cons of each company. During this process we realized that there was a great deal of potential in the local companies that were on the list, and we went back to the club and said that we were going to focus our first "mini–mutual fund" foray on local companies with strong outlooks. We came up with a list which you may or may not have seen on our Web site: MedCath, Food Lion Stores, HFNC Financial (Parent Company of Home Federal Savings, an exemplary S&L), American Studios (purchased by PCA International, another local company).
>
>   In making the decision to focus on local companies we saw an opportunity to educate our members that you have to look no further than your own backyard for good companies with bright futures that make good investments.
>   Paul Kardous, CFO Emeritus

About the NAIC. The National Association of Investors Corp. is the support system of choice for most investment clubs, as well as for hundreds of thousands of individual investors. It offers a catalog of background and materials like accounting manuals, stock selection guides and club documents. And its newsletter is a nice combination of interesting reading and useful tips.

A club membership in NAIC costs thirty-five dollars annually, plus fourteen dollars for each individual member or household. Between the free information and member discounts, it pays for itself several times over.

Informal Venture Capital: The Celestial Choir

They filter into the dining room a little reluctantly, as if the real action is outside in the hall. Most seem to know each other already; they're shaking hands, slapping backs, waving and nodding. Eventually they find seats at the elegantly appointed tables, settling in for what has been billed as "an hour of shameless self-promotion." And sure enough, after some brief preliminaries, entrepreneurs begin to stand up and make quick pitches for newborn businesses ranging from computer leasing to box making to racquetball equipment. In clipped sentences, they explain why they'll succeed, how much capital they'll require, what kind of expertise would be helpful in a patron.

The audience listens more or less attentively, many taking notes. Some, I find out later, are lawyers and accountants, looking for ideas suitable for well-heeled clients. Others are themselves investors, on the prowl for ground-floor opportunities.

All either have serious money to invest or are connected to people who do. This is, in other words, a typical gathering of rich people and their representatives, with but one unusual feature: Not once, in the course of two hours, is there a mention of the stock market.

Welcome to entrepreneurial heaven, otherwise known as a venture capital club, a forum designed to let Bill Gates wanna-bes strut their stuff before a receptive audience of potential investors, or "angels," as they've come to be known.

Informal venture capital—as opposed to the "institutional" kind, which is made up of firms and people who do this for a living—is booming. Why this is so I'll get to in a minute. But the point of mentioning it in a book on growth-stock investing is that it's an even more ideal way to exploit your local advantage. To state the obvious, if you're going to buy into *private* emerging companies, being nearby gives you first crack at the best ideas, and allows you to meet face-to-face with local entrepreneurs and the people who know them and can vouch for their integrity. And it lets you see the results of their past business ventures firsthand.

So, if you're fortunate enough to have a quarter of a million or so to toss around, read on to see if you're angel material. If not, you might still want to consider a venture capital club as the ultimate networking vehicle for local investors. These are the people with the most immediate stake in the local economy. Many of them invest in both public and private companies. And many more of them work for people who do.

Informal venture capital has been around since the first aging hunter traded his spear to a strong-armed youngster in return for a daily chunk of zebra. But in the past decade it's moved out of the shadows and into the mainstream, as a generation of "cashed-out" entrepreneurs begins to use their money and expertise to nurture their successors.

Though figures are imprecise—angels, like most rich people, shun publicity—some studies put the size of the informal venture capital market at around $20 billion annually, or roughly twice what institutional venture capitalists pump into early-stage companies. And because angels tend to invest in smaller increments than venture firms, they seed a vastly greater number of start-ups.

In any given city, then, angels play a major role in new-company formation. A 1994 *Fortune* article put the number of "serious" angels in the Minneapolis/St. Paul area, for instance, at more than sixty, and estimated that they pump more than $200 million a year into the local economy.

In the process, angels are entering financial folklore: There's the New Mexico heiress who funds socially responsible companies run by women; the Loosely Organized Retired Executives (LORE), who finance start-ups around Radnor Township, Pennsylvania; and the McAlester Investment Group, which does the same thing in McAlester, Oklahoma.

Their stories are as different as their hometowns, but all share one characteristic: Shunning formal organizational structure and the major stock exchanges, they're using their accumulated wealth and wisdom to help young entrepreneurs build tomorrow's companies. And many of them are making even bigger fortunes in the process.

The modern age of informal venture capital can be traced

back to 1980, when Carroll Greathouse, an executive with Baxter Associates, a firm that advises nonprofit organizations, drew an assignment to create a venture capital club in Connecticut. "We put the Connecticut Venture Group together and ran it for a while," recalls Greathouse. The club caught on, achieving a measure of success in bringing local entrepreneurs and rich patrons together.

Gradually, word began to spread of the interesting new kind of organization, bigger and more sophisticated than an investment club, more accessible than a venture capital firm. "We started to get publicity—The Wall Street Journal, Venture Economics, Inc.," says Greathouse. "Then we started getting all these inquiries [from others wanting to start similar clubs in other cities]. What are we going to do with all these? We were only interested in what was happening locally."

Rising to the challenge, Greathouse became a sort of patron saint of venture capital clubs. "I took a trip across the country and helped people who had inquired to set up clubs." Then, to nurture and track his creations, he created the International Venture Capital Institute. The institute publishes a directory of venture capital clubs as well as extensive how-to materials, and is now the first stop for would-be club organizers.

While Greathouse was creating this market, William Wetzel was studying it. A professor at the University of New Hampshire's Whittemore School of Business and Economics and a former bank loan officer, Wetzel's interest in informal venture capital was piqued in 1979 when he received a Small Business Administration grant "to test the notion that there's an invisible venture capital market out there that nobody was really aware of, that's populated by self-made, high-net-worth individuals."

He found that there was indeed such a market, and that it was "really the primary source of that first round of outside equity financing that entrepreneurs need once they run through their own money." It was big—though how big he could only guess—and crucially important to the entrepreneurial economy. But at the same time it was "horribly inefficient," with most angels operating in private through their own associates, and most entrepreneurs at a loss when it came to attracting angels' attention.

So Wetzel founded the Center for Venture Research at UNH in the mid-1980s, and spent the next decade trying to sweep the cobwebs from the market's corners. He recently stepped down as head of the center, but it remains the clearinghouse for facts, figures and analyses on angels and their market.

Among the center's findings:

- Because institutional venture capitalists seldom do early-stage, seed-type financing, and in any event seldom invest less than a million dollars, "There's a real hole in the market for entrepreneurs building high-potential-growth businesses when it's early stage and the amount needed is half a million or below." And angels are quietly filling this gap.
- Angels bring know-how as well as capital, and often that's more important than money. They often play an active role, sitting on the board and acting as mentor to the founder. "Angels have the experience to evaluate the merits as well as the risks of the idea," says Wetzel. "In many ways their pro-

fessional careers have prepared them to do the kind of due diligence that any venture capital fund does on a company before they put their money in, because they've lived it."

- Angels prefer to invest close to home. "The odds of an entrepreneur raising capital from an angel rise exponentially the closer they are geographically to the investor."

Joining the Celestial Choir. If this sounds like an interesting variation on Main Street investing, here's a quick course on becoming an angel: Start with money—lots of it. You'll need to be able to put up a minimum of twenty-five thousand dollars into several deals.

Then you'll need contacts. Says Wetzel, "If you find an angel, you've typically found half a dozen, because when they invest they typically do so with their trusted friends and business associates." Like a very sophisticated investment club, such a network allows members to fill the gaps in each others' understanding, and to draw on decades of accumulated experience.

This is crucial, because picking winners and losers at inception is vastly more difficult than picking stocks. "The central mystery of venture capital is how to put a value on a company that has no past and potentially a very exciting future. There are some rational approaches to modeling it, but it remains an art form," says Wetzel. So you're way ahead of the game if you or your associates have a background in the business in question.

To find companies, consider the following:

- *Venture capital clubs,* of course. "When people call me and say, 'Hey I want to invest in some start-ups,' I pay for their lunch and take them to a Connecticut Venture Group meeting," says Carroll Greathouse.

If your town has such a club, that's your logical starting point as well. The club probably sponsors regular meetings, which, for a generally modest fee, are open to the public. They usually feature a speaker who is prominent in the local economy or the world of venture capital. But the main point of the meeting is to network, to put the people with ideas together with those who have money.

- *Business incubators.* Many cities, states and universities have created sheltered environments, usually consisting of a well-wired building or office park, where newborn businesses can find their legs. Business incubators offer cheap rent, shared office equipment and secretaries, and often the advice of more seasoned entrepreneurs. More than six hundred such incubators have sprung up in the United States and Canada in the past fifteen years, with dozens more on the drawing board at any given time.

  Incubators get little publicity, but for angels they tend to be a home away from home. Like Willie Sutton with banks, angels visit incubators because that's where the start-ups are.
- *Venture capital databases.* The holy grail the of the informal venture world is a database containing a confidential list of the angels in an area, which then matches entrepreneurs with the right angels. Sort of a dating service for capital.

  A wonderful idea, but in practice very hard to pull off, given angels' quite legitimate desire for privacy. But because it's so appealing, people keep trying to make it happen. In dozens of cities, local Small Business Administration offices are working with chambers of commerce to set up and computerize angel databases. Once up, they're being linked to others in the region, with the ultimate goal of a nationwide directory of angels and entrepreneurs. In other words, a market in informal venture capital.

A call to your local chamber of commerce can tell you if such a network is operating near you. If the answer is yes, it's worth considering. But because the track record of angel databases is poor, you'll want to investigate before signing on. Ask for references, including a list of deals they've consummated. Unless these are forthcoming and convincing, you may want to wait until the network matures.

If you decide to sign on, the network will ask for proof of your angel credentials—generally some measure of net worth or income. Once you've registered, it will provide you with anonymous summaries of participating entrepreneurs' business plans. If you find one or two you like, you'll be able to call them and start negotiating.

Once you've invested. Getting in on the ground floor magnifies both the risks and the potential rewards of an investment. If the company fails—as most start-ups are destined to—you lose everything. If it succeeds, you can potentially make many times your original stake.

But along the way, succeed or fail, there will be growing pains. First, entrepreneurs are seldom ready for what rapid growth imposes on them, and will need the advice of people who have been there. If that's you, expect to be pulled into the running of the company on some level, either informally or, as is often the case, as an officer.

And also expect to be asked for more money.

If the company runs into trouble, you'll be faced with the dilemma of either providing more cash at the risk of throwing good money after bad or watching as your original investment melts away.

If the company succeeds, it will need expansion capital. To avoid having your original investment diluted by the investors who supply this capital, you should be prepared to put up some of it yourself.

These demands for cash can come suddenly. One start-up is said to have informed its investors on a Wednesday that it would need $500,000 to meet its Friday payroll. The angels found the money, the company survived, and after three years it was estimated to be worth ten times the original investment. But it might have been worth zero if the angels hadn't been there when needed.

How to start your own venture club. Here's an account of the creation of a successful venture capital club in Jacksonville, Florida, in the words of Henry Avery, the club's founder:

> I'm from Boston, an MIT grad. I started a number of companies up there, mostly based on MIT research, and for about 10 years belonged to a [venture] group called 128, which had maybe 200 to 300 members. I was also associated with the Connecticut Venture group.
>
> When I came down here in 1993 I didn't find anything like that. So I asked Carroll Greathouse for a copy of the Connecticut Venture Group's policy manual. He came down and spent a week helping me get organized.
>
> First, we went to the chamber of commerce and they said no. They don't start new businesses. They're in the recruitment business; they spend all their time bringing in $10 million, $20 million, $50 million companies.

I also went to the Small Business Development Group at the University of North Florida Jacksonville. They were not too enthusiastic, even though that's their job.

This is understandable. Money talks; they were always looking for money, and we didn't have any. We'd be using their resources without offering them any grant money.

So I got together a luncheon for ten high-net-worth people, presidents of banks, retirees from big companies. I'm a member of one of the local elite country clubs, where there are a lot of people like that.

[In creating the club's board of directors] I insisted that all these people be businesspeople, not academics or even chamber people. I didn't want negative influences. We now have bank executives, investment bankers, a high-class group of people. Altogether, there are about 150 members.

After I got it all organized, I turned the chairmanship over to someone else and took over the job of finding keynote speakers.

We're set up as a nonprofit organization, so people can donate money for a tax write-off. For $150, you get to attend a breakfast or dinner at one of the best clubs in town. Then we put on a forum every year which attracts a lot of "soft money" [like free ads in the *Jacksonville Business Journal* and cut-rate hotel space].

At every meeting we have a keynote speaker and two entrepreneurial presenters who present their business plans.

I generally get top venture capitalists as speakers. [As for] entrepreneurial presenters, I get a lot of deals on my desk, and I sort through them for the two that look most interesting.

The rest I turn over to people with Avery Associates [his venture capital firm] who have expertise in different fields. I have four or five associates who are specialists in different businesses, including biotech, telecommunications, restaurants and real estate. And I have one guy that takes the trash. I put those in a laundry basket and send them off to him.

If a specialist likes a proposal, he can both invest in it and add it to the First Coast Forum program. There's some question about conflict of interest here because my firm will often have a position in the company. I see nothing wrong with that because the other groups I've been involved in do the same thing.

If we decide to put a proposal on [either the annual forum or a First Coast dinner program], then anyone can invest in it because it's in the public domain.

The average size of an investment is $250,000, though some have been a few million. Usually there's only one investor per deal, and it's generally an angel.

Among First Coast's notable deals:

- "The Edge, which is a way to seal money bags that banks use, to improve security. . . . Six months after we put it on the program, it got a $450,000 investment. Since then it's penetrated most major banks around the country. Now they're doing Las Vegas, where they need lots of security. It's probably up in the millions now."
- "Global Vision, which does laser treatment on eyes. We put that one on two different times. It's gotten around $4 million."

- "Clean Shower, a way to take the mildew out of a bathroom. Our president left to become their vice president. They raised $2 million through us."

Note a few things here. First, the companies that Avery mentions tend to be rather understandable, if a little less glamorous than computers or biotech. Second, each of them, if they succeed, are reasonable candidates for the kind of low-key initial public offering in which local investors make up the bulk of the early interest. So the people who knew these companies when they were private will be the ones who understand them best when they go public.

The Chamber of Commerce

If there's one place where all of the above comes together, it's your local chamber of commerce. This is essentially a networking club for local businesspeople, in which they contrive excuses to exchange business cards. Over the years, chambers have developed some very sophisticated ways to bring their members together, including seminars on various aspects of running a business, early-morning breakfast meetings and awards ceremonies.

Some have research libraries that compile statistics on who does what locally, some publish periodic summaries of the local economy. Most offer information on local companies that has been sorted into various categories.

At a minimum, the chamber is a logical first phone call for people trying to track down many of the other local organiza-

tions mentioned here. If you own or represent a business, joining the local chamber is usually a matter of a few hundred
dollars, most of which can be recouped through all the goodies
they offer, like discounts on local company products, group
health insurance and free business advice.

5

YOUR CITY:
A LABORATORY OF
CAPITALISM

The original design of the United States had the stark, simple beauty of a thing too good to be true. The federal government was to conduct foreign affairs and resolve disputes between the states. And the states were expected to manage their own economic houses. They were forbidden from obstructing interstate commerce and infringing on their citizens' constitutionally enumerated rights, but beyond that, they were free to create the tax and regulatory systems that suited them. Each state was to become a "laboratory of democracy," trying new things, competing and innovating.

In practice, of course, this hasn't always worked. The states have made some truly breathtaking mistakes, and Washington has felt compelled to intervene. In the process, much of economic policy has been nationalized.

But not all of it. States, cities and regions still compete on things like health care, education, financial regulation, environmental laws and taxes. Throw in geographic differences that foster particular industries, and the often random emergence of

dominant companies and industries in one place and not another, and the United States has indeed kept some elements of
the original, decentralized design. States and cities remain lab-
oratories, if not of democracy, then certainly of capitalism. Because of this, cities, regions and states often comprise unique
economic ecosystems, populated by unique economic organ-
isms. Understand what sets your local economy apart, and your
chances of investing successfully go way up.

What follows are four short case studies in how quirks in a
local economy can hand nearby investors a golden opportunity.
In one, the opportunities have passed but the lesson remains a
good one. In two others, the action, as this is written in 1997,
is at its peak. In the fourth, the fun is, maybe, just beginning.

To put these case studies together, I called each region's usual
suspects: local consultants, chamber of commerce officials, brokers and analysts with regional brokerage houses, reporters for
local business journals; the same people whom local investors
can and should call, with the difference being that I'm unlikely
to form long-term relationships with them because I don't live
nearby. Read what follows for lessons that apply to the analysis
of your own local economy: Is a new industry rising nearby? Is
an existing one changing? Is the process creating small companies with promising ideas? If the answer is yes, you've got an
exciting ride ahead of you, and you're on board long before Wall
Street.

Charlotte, North Carolina: Regional Banking's Garden of Eden

One of the more interesting episodes in the earth's history took place around three million years ago, when the long-separate land masses now known as North and South America were joined by the Panamanian land bridge. During their time apart, life on the two continents had evolved in radically different directions. South America was populated by primitive mammals, marsupials and ten-foot-tall, carnivorous, flightless birds, which in artists' renderings look like a cross between an ostrich and T-Rex. North America, meanwhile, was dominated by familiar placental mammals like jaguars and bears.

When the two continents were joined, ecosystems merged and their denizens began competing for a limited set of niches. In only a short time, in evolutionary terms, the North American species drove most southern competitors to extinction. Why this happened is a subject of lively debate among paleontologists, but one theory is that North America had previously been part of a larger "supercontinent" that broke apart before the north-south connection. North American wildlife had thus been exposed to a bigger, more rigorous ecosystem that forced them to become better adapted to their niches, making them better prepared for competition than the creatures of South America. When the opportunity came they made the most of it.

Now let's fast-forward to a very different ecosystem, North Carolina in the 1970s. Back then, the Tar Heel State was relatively poor and only recently desegregated, still a part of the "Old South" in many ways.

It did have one unusual feature, however: very liberal banking laws. Strange as it seems from a 1990s perspective, until recently many states limited their banks to a single branch. As a result, there were few multibranch banking systems, and even fewer that extended across state lines. But since 1814, North Carolina had permitted its banks to establish branches wherever they wanted to. In response, a few entrepreneurs set up multiple-branch chains in towns around the state. Over the course of decades, they and their successors mastered the intricacies of, for instance, tracking charges against the same account originating in different places.

When progress in telecommunications spawned Electronic Funds Transfer (EFT)—which made possible the instantaneous movement of funds between geographically separated branches—North Carolina bankers embraced it. The first automatic teller machine was set up there in 1973; the first credit-card transaction was processed in 1976. The smartest local bankers saw in EFT the possibility of even larger branch networks. So they set up holding companies and began to buy out their competitors. In the process they grew even more adept at managing big, distributed financial services networks. During this time they must have stared hungrily into South Carolina and Virginia, home to dozens of tiny, undercapitalized one-branch banks, and wondered when they would get the chance to spread beyond their own borders. Their chance came in 1984, when a regional, reciprocal interstate banking bill was adopted by a dozen southern states. The law invited banks from each state to invest in North Carolina, in return for which North Carolina would have the same privilege in those states.

And, like jaguars eating their way down to Tierra del Fuego,

North Carolina's three most aggressive banks (which eventually came to be called NationsBank, First Union and Wachovia) began to gobble up the smaller banks in surrounding states. "They were kids in a candy store," recalls a First Union executive. In the decade that followed, NationsBank's assets ballooned from $10 billion to $300 billion, and First Union's from $7 billion to $150 billion. And Charlotte became a financial center—as defined by assets controlled by banks headquartered there—second only to New York City.

That was great news for Charlotte, but even better news for the Big Three's early investors; $1,000 invested in the forerunners of each in 1980 would grow to about $14,000 by mid-1997.

But that's in retrospect, you say. It wouldn't have been clear in 1980 that these three would be the winners. True, *but it wasn't necessary to predict which of North Carolina's banks were going to grow into "superregionals." It was only necessary to identify the process.* Because most of the banks acquired by Charlotte's Big Three were bought for stock rather than cash, you could have accumulated major positions in all three simply by buying a wide selection of small banks in North Carolina. In many cases you would have made a profit on the buyout, then ridden along with the acquirer.

Meanwhile, the predation of the big banks caused countless smaller ones to buy each other out in the hope that size would spell survival. So early investments in some small southern banks went through three or four incarnations before finally becoming NationsBank's lunch. And locals would have noticed first. If you were a North Carolina resident in the seventies and early eighties, chances are your bank was either an acquirer or an acquiree at some point. The local papers, especially in Charlotte but also around the state, published feature articles on bank buyouts and large new bank chains that were being formed (remember, there wasn't a whole lot else going on there at the time). At the very least, the papers noted the parade of bank buyout announcements in prominent parts of their business sections.

There is, however, one flaw in this example: The savings and loan debacle of the late 1980s wiped out many small lenders. This allowed NationsBank to virtually subsume the Texas banking industry, but it also rendered some small-bank stocks worthless. So a secondary lesson here is that security analysis is still crucial, even after you've identified a dominant local trend. A portfolio of takeover-candidate banks would have had to have been chosen for financial strength and stability as well as for location.

Here are lists of the banks acquired by NationsBank and First Union between 1970 and 1996:

Table 5.1
NATIONSBANK

1981
Carolina First National, Lincolnton, NC

1982
First National Bank, Lake City, FL
Gulfstream Banks, Boca Raton, FL
Bancshares of North Carolina, Raleigh, NC
Exchange Ban-Corp., Tampa, FL
Peoples Downtown National, Miami, FL

1984
Ellis Banking Corp., Miami, FL

1985
Pan American Banks, Miami, FL
Southern National Bank, Atlanta, GA

1986
Bankers Trust of South Carolina, Columbia, SC
National Bank, Miami, FL
First American Savings, Gastonia, NC
Southern National, Charlotte, NC
Prince William Bank, Dumfries, VA
Hartsville Bancshares, Hartsville, SC

1987
Panmure Gordon & Co., London, England
CentraBank, Baltimore, MD

1988
U.S. Bancorp, St. Petersburg, FL
First Republic Bank, Dallas, TX
First American Bank, Brevard County, FL

1989
First State Bank, Abilene, TX
Century Savings and Trust, Houston, TX
American Federal Savings, Austin, TX
Great Atlantic Savings, Manteo, NC
First Capital Savings, Houston, TX
Village Savings, Houston, TX
Southern Florida Bank, Boca Raton, FL
University Federal Savings, Houston, TX
Freedom Savings and Loan, Tampa, FL
Greater Texas Bank, Austin, TX

1990
Tyler National, Tyler, TX
Centennial Federal, Greenville, TX
Bankers Savings & Loan, Galveston, TX
First Bank & Trust, Cedar Hill, TX
Meridian Savings Assoc., Arlington, TX
Charles Schreiner Bank, Kerrville, TX

HeritageBank Savings, Duncanville, TX
First National Bank, Georgetown, TX
Carolina Mountain Bank, Highlands, NC
Huntsville National, Huntsville, TX
National Bancshares, San Antonio, TX
East Texas Savings & Loan, Tyler, TX

1991
Commonwealth, Corpus Christi, TX
C&S/Sovran, Atlanta, GA

1993
Chrysler First, Allentown, PA
Chicago Research, Chicago, IL
Maryland National, Baltimore, MD
U.S. West Financial, Englewood, CO

1994
Corpus Christi National, Corpus Christi, TX
California Federal, Los Angeles, CA
Consolidated Bank, Dade County, FL
Cypress Financial, Pasadena, CA
Rock Hill National, Rock Hill, SC

1995
KeyCorp Mortgage, Cleveland, OH
Intercontinental Bank, Dade County, FL
CSF Holdings, Miami, FL
Bank of Madison County, Madison County, FL

1996
Bank South, Atlanta, GA
Citizens Federal, Miami, FL
Sun World Savings, El Paso, TX
LDI Corp., Cleveland, OH
Charter Bancshares, Houston, TX
Source: NationsBank

Table 5.2
FIRST UNION

1981
First National Bank, Catawba County, NC
First National Bank, Albemarle, NC

1982
Salem Securities, Inc., Winston-Salem, NC

1983
Piedmont Corporation, Charlotte, NC

1985
Atlantic Bancorporation, Jacksonville, FL
Northwestern Financial Corp., Greensboro, NC
Central Florida Bank Corp., Dade City, FL

1986
Southern Bancorporation, Greenville, SC
First Bankers Corp., Pompano Beach, FL
The Mall Bank, Palm Beach, FL
Georgia State Bankshares, Atlanta, GA
First Railroad & Banking Co., Augusta, GA
Bank of Waynesboro, Waynesboro, GA

1987
Collier Bank, Naples, FL
Edison Banks, Fort Myers, FL
Rocwell Bank, Roswell, GA
Commerce Bancshares, Naples, FL
First North Port Bancorp, North Port, FL
City Commercial Bank, Sarasota, FL
First Sarasota Bancorp, Sarasota, FL
Sarasota Bank & Trust, Sarasota, FL
First State Bancshares, Pensacola, FL
Community Banking Corp., Bradenton, FL
Bank of Bellevue, Nashville, TN

1988
Florida Commercial Banks, Miami, FL

1990
Florida National Banks of Florida, Jacksonville, FL

1991

Florida Federal Savings, St. Petersburg, FL
Gold Coast Savings Bank, Fort Lauderdale, FL
Southeast Bank, Miami, FL
Southeast Bank of West Florida, Pensacola, FL
American Pioneer, Orlando, FL

1992

Professional Federal Savings Bank, Coral Gables, FL
Flagler Federal Savings and Loan, Miami, FL
Security First Federal Savings and Loan, Daytona Beach, FL
Meritor Savings, Winter Haven, FL
Sailors and Merchants Bank and Trust, Vienna, VA

1993

South Carolina Federal, Columbia, SC
Dominion Bankshares, Roanoke, VA
Georgia Federal Banks, Atlanta, GA
First American Metro, McLean, VA
Enterprise Bank, Winter Park, FL

1994

Jacksonville Federal Savings, Jacksonville, FL
Citizens Federal Savings, Jacksonville, FL
American Bankshares, Monroe, NC
Lieber & Co., Purchase, NY
BancFlorida Financial, Naples, FL
Cobb Federal Savings, Cobb County, GA
Hollywood Federal Savings, Hollywood, FL
Great Western Savings, Tampa, FL

1995

Selected assets of Chase Manhattan in FL
First Florida Savings, Miami, FL
Ameribank Investors, Annandale, VA
Coral Gables Fedcorp, Coral Gables, FL
ABT Mutual Funds, Palm Beach, FL
Rome Federal Savings, Rome, GA
United Financial, Greenwood, SC
Columbia First Bank, Arlington, VA

1996

First Fidelity Bancorporation, Newark, NJ
RS Financial, Raleigh, NC
Brentwood National, Brentwood, TN
Interrail (a leasing company), Chicago, IL
Northbrook Rail Corp, Arlington Heights, IL
Society First Savings, Fort Myers, FL
Center Financial, Waterbury, CT
Home Financial, Hollywood, FL
Boca Raton First National, Boca Raton, FL
Keystone Investments, Boston, MA
Talyor & Clark Insurance, Fairfax,VA

Source: First Union

Nashville: Headquarters of the Health-care Revolution

Ask a hundred people what they know about Nashville and
ninety-nine will say, "Country music." They'll be right, to a
point. The home of the Grand Ole Opry and a thousand recording studios is undeniably the place to be if you want to
become the next Garth Brooks. But for investors, Nashville has
another, less obvious claim to fame: It's the headquarters of the
revolution that's sweeping through America's health-care system. This story begins in the 1960s, when few in the health-
care industry foresaw either the coming crisis or the form of its
resolution, and the dominant system was known as fee-for-
service. Doctors' practices, hospitals and other health-care pro-
viders operated as small, independent businesses. When a
patient visited a doctor, who prescribed whatever he thought
was necessary, the patient's insurance then paid the bill, usually
with no questions asked.

Because neither doctors nor patients had any incentive to care about costs, they—in the aggregate—splurged. Many patients went to the doctor for every ache and sniffle, and some doctors prescribed every test imaginable (in part because they got paid for each one, and in part to protect themselves from the malpractice litigation that grew like a nasty fungus over the whole system).

Hospitals, meanwhile, found that in order to attract patients, they first had to attract doctors. And this required that they have the latest high-tech equipment, regardless of how much it cost or how infrequently it was used. So they felt compelled to buy MRIs, CAT scanners and lasers by the truckload, all paid for by the insurance companies, who then raised rates to cover the skyrocketing costs. The result was an upward spiral in health-care costs. By 1996 Americans were spending more than $1 trillion, or about 14 percent of GDP, on health care each year, even though one citizen in eight lacked insurance. And 40% of hospital beds were unoccupied, a level of excess capacity that would cripple any other industry.

Now, when a field is this fragmented and inefficient, far-sighted entrepreneurs usually try to "consolidate" it by buying up a bunch of small players and melding them into a big, highly efficient network. This more advanced organism then drives most of the remaining little guys to extinction by offering lower prices, better service and/or a wider selection. In medicine, the new, more efficient organism is the Health Maintenance Organization, or HMO, a combination doctor's office, hospital and insurance company. Instead of getting paid for each service it delivers, it gets a set fee per patient per year, a method known as capitation. For this fee, the HMO agrees to meet its patients' health-care needs, whatever they may be. Because it keeps whatever it doesn't spend on a given patient, an HMO is motivated to hold down costs by doing only what's necessary, and by doing it in the most efficient way.

That's where Nashville comes in. Back in 1968, two local doctors teamed up with a venture capitalist (whose prior claim to fame was taking Kentucky Fried Chicken public) to create Hospital Corporation of America.

Their goal was to buy up hospitals and run them like efficient businesses. They would use their size to cut better deals with suppliers, standardize operating practices and attract high-volume business from corporate health plans and insurance companies. And, where possible, they would merge hospitals with excess capacity into single units that could operate flat out.

This worked beyond anyone's expectations, and by the end of 1996, the now merged and renamed Columbia/HCA owned 340 hospitals and employed 270,000 people, more than either GM or IBM. To manage its growth, HCA had gathered to its Nashville headquarters the best and brightest of this generation's health-care iconoclasts. Once inside, they began doing what bright middle managers in fast-changing industries have always done: leave and start their own companies.

Check out HCA's "family tree" in table 5.3 and you'll see that, one way or another, the company has spawned a total of forty-five other firms, most of them in and around Nashville. Prominent examples include PhyCor, which owns and runs physician practices across the country, National Healthcare and

American Home Patient, which are consolidating the hot, fragmented home-health-care business, and OrNda, which is a smaller but faster growing version of Columbia/HCA.

As of mid-1996, fourteen of Nashville's health-care companies were publicly traded. Together they generated sales of better than $22 billion, but—here's why this matters to local investors—eight of them had sales of less than $300 million, making them too small for widespread out-of-town recognition. And the process is accelerating. According to an article in a 1996 edition of *Economic Edge*, a publication of the Tennessee Valley Authority, even industry insiders can't keep up: "The number of health-care companies in town ranges from 100 to 200, but a reliable count just isn't possible, because new businesses are started and existing ones acquired almost weekly."

The article notes that in the eighteen months ending June 1996, venture capitalists poured more than $300 million into Nashville health-care start-ups. That, estimates the Nashville Health Care Council, was four out of every ten venture capital dollars devoted to health care nationally. In fact, the appetite for new, innovative health-care companies is so great that local health-care execs now get frequent calls at home from venture capitalists asking them to quit their jobs and start their own companies.

Some recent examples of how this torrent of cash lubricates the process: After losing his job with Surgical Care Affiliates when it was bought out, the company's ex-president quickly put together $20 million and founded a chain of women's health clinics called Symmetry Health Partners. And after Columbia/HCA bought out hospital chain Healthtrust, three former ex-

Table 5.3
NASHVILLE'S HEALTH-CARE FAMILY TREE
Hospital Corporation of America

Spinoffs	Headed or founded by former HCA officials	Previously owned by HCA	Financed by HCA
Allied Clinical Labs	American Service Group	Surgical Care Affiliates	Massey Burch Invest. Group
HCA International	Cumberland Health Systems	HealthSouth	Franklin Venture Capital
Quorum Health	MedShares Home Care	Wessex	Richland Ventures
HealthTrust	Riverndell	American HomePatient	
Clayton Associates	IPN Network	Advocat	
Arcon HealthCare	Pinnacle Care		
American Pathology Resources	National Imaging Affiliates		
OrNda HealthCorp.	Gene Burton & Associates		
NetCare Health Systems	Health Care Property Investors		
New American Healthcare	Buyers Healthcare Cooperative		
Gordian Health Solutions	American Transitional Hospitals		
Health Info Technics	Behavioral Healthcare		
Vivra Health Advantage	PhyCor		
UniPhy Healthcare	OrthoLink		
LifeTrust America	Renal Care Group		
HealthCare Facilities Planning	Long Term Care Physicians		
	Women's Health Partners		
	Pain Care		
	Phoenix Healthcare		
	Statcorp		
	Practice Resource Network		

Source: Nashville Health Care Council

ecutives launched three new companies in the space of one month.

Most of this party is going on outside Wall Street's spotlight, because it's happening too fast and the players are too small. Major brokerage house health-care analysts, for instance, cover only twenty or thirty large companies, and so don't have the time to follow Nashville's new-company-every-week frenzy. And without the support of brokerage house research, most out-of-town money managers are clueless when it comes to small Nashville IPOs. But locally there's information in abundance. The *Nashville Business Journal* publishes a weekly stocks section that highlights both new issues and fast-moving stocks. Both the *Journal* and *The Nashville Tennessean*, the city's general-interest newspaper, run frequent stories profiling the major players and alerting readers to pending IPOs. As for local brokerage houses, the *Nashville Business Journal* publishes an annual listing of the city's largest brokerage houses, part of which is reproduced on page 42. There you'll find four, and maybe six, brokerage houses that focus on stocks in the Nashville area. Equitable Securities, for instance, has forty-seven brokers and has been in town since 1930. Wiley Brothers has forty-five reps and has been there since 1945.

You can bet that each of them has veteran analysts, investment bankers and brokers whose careers are built around local health care. They belong to the same exclusive clubs as local health-care entrepreneurs, they play golf together, their kids attend the same schools and their spouses see each other socially. When something exciting happens nearby, they hear about it first, often because they're involved in it.

Another source is the Nashville Health Care Council, an organization that, among other things, tries to bring investors and entrepreneurs together. The council operates a Web site at http://www.healthcarecouncil.com, and publishes extensive data on who's doing what around town.

So forget country music. Nashville, crows Laura Ortale, executive director of the Health Care Council, "is the health care capital of the world."

D.C.'s Virginia Suburbs: Silicon Valley East?

If, say, a decade ago you had been asked to guess where the next Silicon Valley would spring up, your list of possibilities would probably have included frontier towns, like Portland and Santa Fe. It's a safe bet that Washington, D.C.'s Virginia suburbs would not have come to mind; too close to the bureaucracy, with too high a ratio of lawyers to engineers and too few elite universities, Alexandria, Reston and Vienna hardly seemed the kind of towns where entrepreneurism would take hold.

And yet, in a classic case of unintended consequences, D.C.'s Virginia burbs have emerged in the past few years as one of the most dynamic markets for high-tech start-ups in the country. This boom created several dozen new millionaires in 1996, and, if the local players are right in their predictions, will produce twice that many in 1997, and more again in 1998.

To understand how it happened, let's begin with the Pentagon's 1960s realization that future battles would be won by the side best able to keep track of who was blowing up what. That meant telecommunications systems "robust" enough to survive the stress of battle, and computers capable of sharing data across considerable distances. So the Department of Defense called in the industrial half of the military-industrial complex and asked them to design and build such a system. Version one, called DARPANET, for Defense Advanced Research Projects Agency, went on-line in 1969. By today's standards a rudimentary network of land lines connecting slow computers at universities and defense contractors, it was still a revelation to its early users. They immediately saw the value of being wired and encouraged the evolution of DARPANET into other, slicker systems, one of which eventually became the Internet.

Now, from just about any angle, the defense contractors who built DARPANET were the antithesis of emerging growth. Toiling in suburban D.C. obscurity on low-margin cost-plus contracts, they built esoteric things that no one in that era's private sector cared about. But beneath the lackluster façade, a generation of technicians was grasping the implications of things like advanced switching and network-based interactive communication. Years before the rest of us had even heard the term Internet, these guys were thinking about how to build it, run it and profit from it.

So, when the World Wide Web brought humanity on-line in 1993, there, in northern Virginia, were hundreds of people who knew what we needed. And they started acting just like Nashville's health-care revolutionaries, leaving to start their own companies. Then they started selling stock.

It began as a trickle in 1994, with public offerings from technology firms like Transaction Network Services and Coherent

Communications, then gained visibility with high- profile Internet access suppliers like UUNet and PSI. Their success, in
turn, drew the attention of the other players necessary for a full-
fledged boom. New venture capital firms like Novak Biddle and
Blue Water Capital were formed, and established players like
New Enterprise Associates and AT&T Ventures moved into the
area. Once in place, they began showering start-up capital on
would-be entrepreneurs.

At the other end of the pipeline, investment banks like D.C.-
based Ferris Baker Watts and Friedman, Billings, Ramsey began
hiring technology expertise and vying for the chance to take the
successful start-ups public. Friedman, Billings, Ramsey, especially, is an object lesson in the interaction of an investment
bank and its environment. Founded by former employees of local investment bank Johnson Lemon, its initial focus was on
small banks. FBR underwrote its first initial public offering in
the spring of 1994—for Prime Retail Group, a real estate investment trust.

But it soon dawned on FBR management that telecommunications and computers were revolutionizing the banking
business, and to understand banking, the firm had to understand
technology. In response, it brought in analysts and investment
bankers who knew the field. And in just the past two years, it
has become a major underwriter of northern Virginia technology IPOs. Now FBR is starting its own venture capital fund,
Pegasus Partners.

The result of this confluence of knowledge and money
has been an explosion of initial public offerings. In the eighteen months ending May 1, 1997, twenty-four companies went

public in northern Virginia's 703 area code, versus a total of ten for the rest of the state. In the aggregate, they raised $831 million.

What these companies do is as interesting as the wealth they're creating. There's UOL Publishing, a pioneer in on-line learning, which converts popular classroom material to Web-based, interactive learning programs; n-Vision, which makes and sells state-of-the-art virtual reality gear; and Apache Medical Systems, a leader in the kind of "decision support information systems for the health-care industry" that's driving down costs and raising efficiency in an industry that sorely needs it. The list goes on—see pages 279–281 (northern Virginia's entry in the IPO list) for an idea of just how far.

Now, say participants, the real fun begins. "The people who work for [recent IPOs] get paid to a degree in stock options," says the head of a public relations firm that represents a number of northern Virginia start-ups. These suddenly rich people "have the entrepreneurial attitude, and they have their own seed capital. So they're going out and creating their own businesses. So not only is wealth being created here, but the engine that creates more wealth is being created here."

The result: even more IPOs in the pipeline. "We like to think of the D.C. metropolitan area, and really down through Virginia and into North Carolina, as the next Silicon Valley," says Friedman, Billings, Ramsey's top investment banker. "You're going to see more companies in this region go public in the second half of this year than you did in all of 1996, and then in 1998, you'll double that again."

If you're in northern Virginia and you'd like a piece of this newly created wealth, a logical place to begin is with the three papers that cover the region: *The Washington Post*, of course, has a world-class business section, and the *Washington Business Journal* and *Washington Technology* both do a good inside job of following recent and pending IPOs and profiling new local companies. Several brokerage houses also now specialize, more or less, in northern Virginia stocks. Among them are Legg-Mason; Ferris Baker Watts; Wheat First; and Scott & Stringfellow.

And don't overlook public relations companies. Small companies find it hard to get favorable press in the general cacophony, so they often hire PR firms like Poretz Group and Geddings Communications to help get the word out. These firms are prejudiced in favor of their clients, of course, but they have tons of background material at their disposal, and can also put you in touch with other people who have useful insights.

Detroit: Tomorrow's Growth Stock Mecca?

Detroit should be an easy one. Because it's dominated by General Motors, Ford and Chrysler, you'd expect it to feature a smorgasbord of hot little public companies selling parts and services to the local giants. In any event, the auto industry is nearly a century old, so Detroit's investment scene should long since have coalesced into a stable form, right?

Wrong on both counts. As this is written in 1997, there are only a handful of Detroit-based transportation firms that fall into the "emerging, public" category. But some astute local observers think that's about to change. In fact, they say, the Motor

City may be poised for a transformation from emerging growth backwater to IPO hot spot.

Detroit has been synonymous with cars since 1913, when Henry Ford's Highland Park assembly line began turning out an unheard of one thousand cars a day. His innovation was copied by others, and the auto industry entered the mass market. And Detroit entered folklore as America's Motor City. In many ways the early days of the auto industry resembled the 1980s personal computer business, with dozens of companies springing up to build a revolutionary new machine. Some flourished, but the vast majority either disappeared or were swallowed up by more successful rivals until, with Chrysler's acquisition of American Motors, there were three.

Still, the community of firms that supply the auto makers with brakes, windshields and chrome trim remained highly fragmented, because that's the way the auto makers liked it.

Traditionally, the Big Three would put a job out for bid, and let a swarm of little suppliers compete on price for parts of it. This created hundreds of niches for small players capable of producing a single piece of larger systems. And today, as a result, dozens of auto-related companies generate sales in the $25 million to $100 million range. Some are highly profitable, some are growing quickly, but few are available to investors. In fact, publicly held companies—i.e., those with stock you can buy—make up less than 5 percent of Detroit's auto-supplier population, according to one recent study.

Why aren't the owners of these companies selling stock to the public, like rational entrepreneurs? It's a combination of several things, say observers.

First, auto parts—and transportation in general—is seen by Wall Street as low-tech and therefore low-growth, which makes it a hard sell to investors.

Second, most of the Big Three's suppliers are run by midwestern entrepreneurs who are more interested in building a life than in cashing out. Their "exit strategy" is more likely to involve an undertaker than an IPO. Hence, they're willing to forego outside capital to preserve their independence.

Third, technology is revolutionizing materials science, factory operations and component design, making it harder than ever to predict which of the Big Three's small suppliers will thrive.

And finally, the auto industry has been in turmoil for two decades. The Japanese invasion and oil shocks of the 1970s transformed the Big Three from rulers of the transportation world to impotent giants whose survival, for a while there, was uncertain. In order to compete, they began adopting the methods of their foreign competitors. They're outsourcing many jobs that previously were done in-house with expensive UAW labor. And they're redefining the relationship between auto maker and parts supplier. Instead of shifting alliances based on price, the Big Three now want long-term, intimate relationships with fewer suppliers.

The result: Many small suppliers are being squeezed out, while those that survive are attracting huge orders. But as this is happening, it's not at all clear which suppliers will survive and in what form. This, as much as anything else, makes Wall Street leery of betting on auto-parts companies in general. As one auto industry consultant puts it, "For the last couple of years, the business risk has been perceived as being very high because of all the consolidation. This has driven down earnings multiples for transactions. So until recently there were more sellers than buyers because no one knew which companies would survive."

So it's not all that surprising that only one in twenty of the companies serving the Big Three are publicly traded.

But that's about to change. The supplier community is reacting to the Big Three's new attitude by consolidating. That is, they're merging with or selling out to each other in an effort to create big, stable companies likely to be chosen as partners by the auto makers.

One favorite strategy is the "product rollup," in which a company acquires the ability to make all the pieces of a given system. Says the previously quoted consultant, "By buying a cable company, a lever assembly company and a caliper company and rolling them up into one, I can make a company that can develop, design, engineer and manufacture a total parking brake system." This "has a lot of appeal" to the investment community, because such a company can cut costs and generate economies of scale on large contracts. It can, in short, make a lot of money.

Though based in Minneapolis, Tower Automotive is an oft-cited example of where Detroit's metal benders are headed. Instead of stamping out simple things like hood hinges, it's spent the past few years buying up companies that do such things, and now makes its money by combining these components into complex, value-added products. Its revenues rose from $81 million in 1992 to $360 million in 1996. And in January 1997 it agreed to an acquisition that will triple its size. "A pure supplier consolidation play," concludes one local brokerage house analyst.

The second driver of Detroit's coming growth-stock boom is technology. The computer and material science revolutions are, finally, flowing into the car business, creating all kinds of niches for new products and processes. Among the cool things on the horizon are night-vision capabilities, computerized navigation aids, speech-based driver interfaces, more efficient batteries and alternative fuel engines. Meanwhile, supercomputers and PC networks promise to remake the manufacturing process in ways that can only be guessed at today.

This combination of fast, unpredictable change and a huge potential market is turning the staid auto industry into the kind of environment that visionary entrepreneurs love. Start-ups will begin to flourish, and Wall Street will pay attention. Take, for example, Gentex. Originally in the fire-detection business, Gentex adapted its technology to create automatic-dimming mirrors, which have caught on as standard or optional equipment on several vehicles. Gentex's technology is both patented and highly valued by consumers, a potent combination for Wall Street, which made the stock one of 1996's success stories.

With many more Towers and Gentexes in the pipeline, smart money is starting to flow into transportation stocks once again. "We're seeing a lot more money available than there are good deals to be had," says yet another observer. And that is a classic precursor to an IPO boom.

For Detroit residents who want to participate, here are three sources of information:

- Roney & Co. is a Detroit-based investment bank and brokerage house that has two analysts and several investment bankers covering the transport industry full-time. Some of the above, in fact, was drawn from Roney's frequent special reports on trends within the industry. These guys are likely to be in on the best deals (or at least aware of the ones that got away) and will almost certainly have a better handle on Detroit's emerging market than will analysts based in New York or Los Angeles. Open an account with one of Roney's veteran brokers, and you're immediately tied into this stream of ideas.

- *Crain's Detroit Business*, which has been covering the auto industry for nearly two decades, has two reporters who do nothing but look for interesting stories in transportation. "We cover the little companies that no one else follows," says a *Crain's* editor. And readers with questions are encouraged to call. "I wouldn't feel comfortable about a reporter giving investment information or talking about things that aren't yet published," says the editor. "But they can give out the names of other people who might be good sources."

   Crain's also has a Web site that gives E-mail access to every reporter. "A good reporter is on the phone all day long so it's hard to reach them, but via E-mail you can ask a question and get a quick response," says the editor.

- And, last but not least, the Detroit Chamber of Commerce is full of good ideas. I began my search with a call to the chamber's research library, which put me in touch with several of the people who supplied the background for this chapter. It was that easy.

6

A LOCAL COMPANY
LIFE CYCLE

For proof that local sources give you an advantage over Wall Street, simply take a successful company and look at the information that was available on it during its rise. You're likely to find that the company was the subject of frequent articles in its local paper and aggressive coverage by nearby brokerage houses long before it made a splash nationally.

I recently spent an afternoon rooting through the archives of one such company (whose public relations staff had the foresight to save every press clipping and brokerage house report published on it since its inception). The result is something every individual investor should see.

Markel Corp. is a specialty insurance company headquartered in Richmond, Virginia. A decade ago it hit on the idea of focusing on small, narrow, hard-to-insure niches like racehorses and karate studios. By studying the risks involved in these businesses, it's able to price its insurance more accurately than full-line competitors. More accurate pricing means fewer underwriting losses and a more predictable profit. Not to mention, the company is quick to point out, the satisfaction of serving clients who normally have trouble buying insurance.

This strategy has worked beautifully: Since 1990, Markel's premium income has grown steadily. Its stock price, meanwhile, rose tenfold between 1990 and 1996.

But besides its obvious success, Markel is an unusually good example of local advantage for several reasons. First, the insurance business bores most people. So, without a compelling "hook," national publications seldom feature small insurance companies from the hinterlands.

Second, the insurance industry is already dominated by an array of giants. So mutual funds and other institutional investors already have plenty of familiar, easy-to-trade choices if they decide to move money into this sector. Small newcomers—even those with good stories—have a hard time getting noticed.

Third, because insurance companies make most of their money by investing policyholder premiums, they tend to have massive investment portfolios that produce big, unpredictable capital gains. This makes their quarterly income erratic, often producing down earnings year-over-year because the prior year had a big capital gain. So understanding the underlying trends requires reading beyond the headlines, which for most of us means access to frequent updates and analyses.

Add it all up, and you get a company that can do big things for a long time before anyone outside the immediate area cares.

So here's what the afternoon of research turned up: Markel was taken public in 1987 by two large out-of-state brokerage houses. The underwriters did their initial quite favorable reports, and promised ongoing coverage. "But we heard very little from them after that," recalls a Markel spokesman. In the ensuing years, Markel did get a smattering of national press: It was written up in two insurance-industry magazines; it was also mentioned in *Investor's Business Daily*'s "New America" section, a *Forbes* column on momentum stocks and a *Wall Street Journal* list of earnings surprises. But that's it, nationally, over a span of fifteen years.

Meanwhile, information was pouring out nearby. The numbers on chart 6.1 note when a piece of local publicity, either a newspaper or magazine article or a report by a local brokerage house, was published. (An itemized list follows the chart.)

What you see here, by the way, represents less than half of what was actually published. For brevity's sake—you probably won't read all this as it is—I've listed representative examples, and have skipped the many instances where one event was chronicled in several local forums.

As you go along, note two things in particular: During the recession of 1990, Markel's earnings growth stalled, along with that of the overall insurance industry, and its stock price fell by about 50 percent. But instead of abandoning it, local brokerage houses, whose analysts knew Markel's management and understood the company's strengths, maintained coverage. And they began recommending the stock at the bottom.

Meanwhile, during the worst of the downturn, the local papers were dutifully printing earnings reports and quoting local brokerage house analysts about the company's prospects.

A second crucial period for local investors was when Markel began taking large capital gains from its investment portfolio. This happened several times in the early 1990s, causing down quarters that probably turned off many investors who screen for things like earnings momentum, or who simply scan earnings reports and reject companies with negative year-over-year comparisons. But readers of the local paper and clients of local brokerages houses got the full story. Reporters and analysts frequently pointed out that the distortion was due to capital gains and that underlying insurance operations continued to grow.

Chart 6.1
LOCAL COVERAGE OF MARKEL CORP.

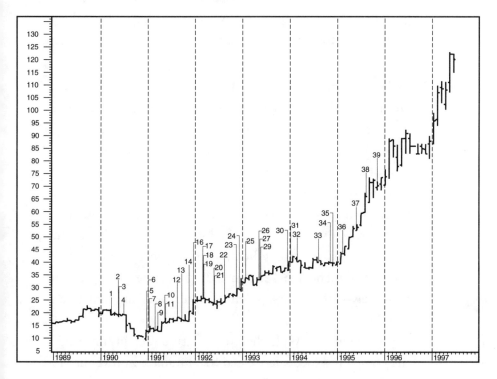

1. *Richmond News Leader*, April 23, 1990.
   "Investment Advice": The article excerpts a report by Richmond-based brokerage house Scott & Stringfellow, noting,

among other things, that the analyst was raising his earnings estimate for Markel in 1990.

The analyst asserts that the improvement is actually greater than the reported 8 percent because "our estimate reflects higher-quality earnings than those reported last year." The report rated the shares a buy for aggressive investors.

2. *Richmond News Leader*, May 14, 1990.

"Markel posts earnings gain of 4 percent during first quarter": The article notes that operating revenues jumped 43 percent due to an acquisition, while pretax income was down slightly due to lower investment income.

3. *Richmond News Leader*, May 17, 1990.

"Markel reaffirms long-term focus": A report on the previous day's annual meeting, where Markel officials "reaffirmed their commitment to long-term growth, even at the cost of short-term profits."

The article quotes Markel's chairman as saying that the recent acquisition of a large competitor cut the past quarter's earnings, but will pay off in the long run by broadening the product line and strengthening the company's position in important niche markets, including summer camps, boys clubs, day-care centers, private schools and community centers.

It concludes: "While the profit picture remains uncertain, the company expects to exceed $100 million in revenues for the first time this year."

4. Davenport & Co., a Richmond-based brokerage house.

Report dated June 26, 1990: The analyst predicts steady

earnings gains in the next two years, and points out that the P/E ratio on projected 1991 earnings is 6.2, low even for the insurance business. His conclusion: "We recommend Markel Corp. . . . to aggressive investors seeking long-term capital gains."

5. *Richmond News Leader*, December 19, 1990.
"Markel makes deals to tighten focus": The article offers an overview of the company's acquisition of one insurer and sale of stakes in two others. It quotes Markel management as saying that the deals will simplify its structure and strengthen its specialty insurance business.
In the previous six months, Markel's stock had declined by about 50 percent, and its market capitalization had fallen to about $60 million.

6. *Richmond Times-Dispatch*, January 1, 1991.
A brief article quoting a local brokerage house analyst: "Markel's earnings have very positive momentum. We predict earnings per share of $2.55 in 1991 will be followed by $3 in 1992, and we believe that Markel can earn $5 plus in a few years. We view Markel shares as undervalued at current levels and look for a multiple expansion as Markel demonstrates that its restructuring has been successful."

7. Scott & Stringfellow.
Report dated 1/7/91: "Markel . . . has just completed a strategic evolution by which the company has taken steps to streamline operations, and incidentally make itself more easily understood by the investment community."
The report notes a slight decline in earnings in the just completed 1990, and predicts a slight increase in 1991, and

notes that the insurance market is weak, and not yet notice-
ably improving.

The analyst also notes that Markel had two problems:
First, the insurance industry is down, and second, the company's reports are hard to analyze because of its many un-
consolidated subsidiaries. "The recent restructuring should
alleviate these problems to some extent." Rating: Hold.

8. *Richmond News Leader*, February 26, 1991.
"Markel lists declines for quarter, year": Charges related to
the restructuring and shedding of several discontinued operations caused a loss in the fourth quarter. The article goes
on to say that continuing operations made money, and that
the prior year's acquisitions resulted in a 52 percent increase
in revenues and a better than tripling of assets.

9. Davenport & Co.
Report dated March 15, 1991: "We recommend the purchase of Markel Corp. in aggressive accounts seeking long-
term capital appreciation . . ." The report makes the
following points:

Earnings leverage has been greatly increased. Markel
could earn $4 to $5 a share by 1995. Cash flow should be
way up as well.

The past year's restructuring has focused the company on
areas where it is strong.

A simpler corporate structure will be easier to manage.

Insiders at Markel own a substantial amount of stock,
which provides a powerful motivation to make the new corporate structure work.

Markel's market cap: $77 million.

10. *Richmond Times-Dispatch*, May 9, 1991.

    "Sales, earnings increase sharply at Markel Corp.": A brief article detailing a big jump in Markel's first quarter results. Earnings were up 62 percent, about twice analysts' estimates, while revenue was triple the year ago figure.

11. Scott & Stringfellow.

    Report dated May 14, 1991: "Markel appears to have completed its "strategic evolution" and is now focused entirely on marketing and underwriting specialty insurance. We have been hesitant about recommending these shares until we could see how the company ultimately would be structured. To this point, we like what we see. . . . We believe the company is capable of producing earnings and cash flow numbers that make the current price appear very attractive. . . . This might allow Markel to command a price in the mid-to-upper $20s within a year."

12. Davenport & Co.

    Report dated August 12, 1991: "We continue to recommend that aggressive investors purchase these shares for long-term capital appreciation . . . an impressive level of earnings leverage . . . an improving balance sheet, and a strong management team with a large vested interest."

    Markel's market cap: $99 million.

13. Scott & Stringfellow.

    Report dated September 16, 1991: "Last week Markel management made a presentation to the Richmond Society of Financial Analysts. Recognizing that one major hurdle that the company has had to overcome is the perception that their business is confusing, MAKL addressed that issue in a concise and informative manner. We will attempt to convey their remarks because we rate this stock a strong buy and believe that to understand it is to recognize a great opportunity."

The report goes on to outline Markel's business and to predict dramatic gains in earnings and cash flow.

14. *Richmond News Leader*, November 11, 1991.
"Markel reports net income rise through nine months": Operating revenues more than tripled and net income rose by 25 percent.

15. Davenport & Co.
Report dated November 11, 1991: The report reiterates the buy recommendation and updates clients on the most recent earnings figures.

16. *Richmond News Leader*, December 16, 1991.
The article quotes from a new buy recommendation by Branch, Cabell & Co., a Richmond-based brokerage house: "In our opinion, Markel has transformed itself at an opportune time and is in a position to benefit dramatically when the underwriting cycle turns favorable."

17. Scott & Stringfellow.
Report dated February 27, 1992: "Just when you thought they were making things simple, there they go again." The report attempts to sort out the complexities of Markel's recent earnings report, including charges from discontinued operations, gains from sales of subsidiaries and several re-

statements of past results. "We recognize that Markel continues to be confusing and that the latest report was more confusing than most. However, we believe management is creating a strong, well-defined and eventually easily understandable money generating machine."

Markel's market cap: $130 million.

18. *Kleos Magazine*, March 1, 1992.
Kleos compiles slick corporate profiles in magazine article format and mails them to local business leaders. It produced a flattering two-page piece on Markel, and sent it to several thousand local executives.

19. Davenport & Co.
Report dated March 3, 1992: The analyst raises his year-ahead earnings estimate on the strength of better underwriting results, and reiterates the strong buy recommendation for aggressive accounts.

20. Davenport & Co.
Report dated May 20, 1992: Reiterates the strong buy.

21. *Richmond Times-Dispatch*, May 22, 1992.
"Annual Meeting": The article consists of an 8½-by-4-inch box noting Markel's annual meeting and reviewing the dramatic jump in 1991 earnings. It also quotes a Markel executive to the effect that "1992 is off to a very good start," with net income up 147 percent year-over-year.

22. *Richmond Times-Dispatch*, August 12, 1992.
"Markel posts 39% gain in profits": A synopsis of the company's second-quarter earnings.

23. Davenport & Co.

Report dated November 11, 1992: Notes that third-quarter earnings were below year-ago levels, but that the previous year was inflated by an accounting adjustment. Because operating earnings were slightly below expectations, the analyst scales back year-ahead estimates by a few cents. He retains the buy recommendation.

24. Scott & Stringfellow.

Report dated December 4, 1992: "We continue to recommend Markel for long-term oriented capital gains investors." The analyst predicts that even in a sluggish environment Markel's strategy will produce much higher earnings, and that in good times, "earnings could be rather stronger indeed."

He predicts that earnings will grow at a 26 percent rate through 1995. "A market multiple of 15 times earnings would suggest a price in 1995 of $90 a share."

Markel stock is $28, its market cap $145 million.

25. *Richmond Times-Dispatch*, January 24, 1993.

"Acquisitions begin to pay dividends": The story discusses the success several Richmond companies—including Markel—were having with aggressive acquisition strategies.

26. Davenport & Co.

Report dated March 4, 1993: Reiterates the buy recommendation.

Markel has risen to $35, and now has a market cap of $182 million.

27. *Richmond Times-Dispatch*, May 11, 1993.

    "Markel reports strong first quarter": Earnings were actually down by more than 50 percent, but the article points out that this was due to the sale the previous year of two major divisions for a large gain. "Without those two items, first quarter net income more than doubled this year."

28. *Richmond Times-Dispatch*, May 11, 1993.

    "Markel Corp. earnings soar in 3rd quarter": The article highlights a 37 percent jump in quarterly results, and again explains that the prior year's profit was inflated by non-recurring items.

29. *Richmond Times-Dispatch*, May 19, 1993.

    "Annual Meeting": An 8½-by-4-inch box announcing Markel's annual meeting, complete with earnings table showing a big recent increase and a "Year Ahead" section noting that first-quarter earnings from continuing operations doubled.

30. Robinson-Humphrey.

    The Atlanta-based brokerage house initiates coverage of Markel with a twelve-page report dated December 12, 1993: "A recent visit with Richmond, Virginia-based Markel Corporation has boosted our enthusiasm for this well-managed specialty property-casualty insurance company. Over the past two years, Markel has successfully transitioned from a diversified broker and underwriter of niche insurance coverage to an underwriter almost exclusively. . . . We rate MAKL a strong long-term buy for aggressive accounts.

    Market cap: $211 million.

31. Scott & Stringfellow.
    Report dated January 3, 1994: Reiterates the buy recommendation, and estimates that earnings will rise to $4.50 a share in 1994, from $2.74 in 1992.
    Market cap: $240 million.

32. *Richmond Times-Dispatch*, February 20, 1994.
    "Operating income rises 75% at Markel."

33. *Richmond Times-Dispatch*, August 5, 1994.
    The article notes that Markel's earnings fell year-over-year, but subtracting out sales of investments, they actually rose strongly.

34. *Richmond Times-Dispatch*, November 2, 1994.
    Markel's reported earnings fell, but its operating profit rose strongly again.

35. Scott & Stringfellow.
    Report dated November 21, 1994: The analyst predicts earnings growth of 51 percent in the coming year, and reiterates his buy recommendation.

36. Robinson-Humphrey.
    Report dated February 10, 1995: Updates 1994's results, and reiterates the buy recommendation.

37. Scott & Stringfellow.
    Report dated May 23, 1995: Reiterates the buy, projects another big earnings increase in 1996.
    Market cap: $300 million.

38. *Richmond Times-Dispatch*, August 8, 1995.
    "Markel profits soar": A brief article noting an earnings increase of 82 percent in the June quarter.

39. *Richmond Times-Dispatch*, October 31, 1995.
    "Jump in third quarter profit sends Markel's stock soaring."
    Market cap: $414 million.

7

SECURITY ANALYSIS: COMPOSING THE STORY

The first half of this book covered the why and how of finding local companies. Let's say you've taken some of that advice and turned up a dozen or so firms that fit the general profile of "small, fast-growing and obscure." Now it's time to winnow the list down to the handful with real long-term potential.

Because security analysis is already the subject of a mountain of literature, much of it available at your local bookstore, I won't attempt anything comprehensive or especially original here. Instead, this chapter and the one that follows will sketch out an *approach* to understanding and valuing the emerging local companies you find.

Not surprisingly, one approach that's both logical and accessible comes from Peter Lynch. In *One Up on Wall Street,* he asks his readers to compose a company's "story," by first fitting it into a general category, then deciding what makes it unique, and then figuring out which numbers are the best indicators of its continued health.

Here's how Lynch does it for a favorite growth stock:

La Quinta is a motel chain that started out in Texas. It was very profitable there. The company successfully duplicated its successful formula in Arkansas and Louisiana. Last year it added 20 percent more motel units than the year before. Earnings have increased every quarter. The company plans rapid future expansion. The debt is not excessive. Motels are a low-growth industry, and very competitive, but La Quinta has found something of a niche. It has a long way to go before it has saturated the market.

The language is simple and the concepts clear. But a lot of information is nevertheless being conveyed: For La Quinta's story to remain intact, it has to (1) keep adding new motels aggressively, (2) without overly leveraging itself, while (3) continuing to earn more money each quarter. This, in turn, points you to several key financial indicators, including the rate of motel additions, sales growth at existing motels (known as same-store sales), profit margins and the debt/equity ratio. When they change, so does the story.

Composing the Story

Companies, like people, come in all shapes, sizes and types. But, again as with people, some types seem to recur so frequently that understanding them gives you a shortcut to judging them, or at least leads you to the relevant questions.

Among the emerging growth stocks I've spent the past few years following, five types that appear most frequently are:

The consolidator. This is a company that finds a "fragmented" niche, i.e., a business that's populated by a bunch of small (often referred to as "mom and pop") operators. Then it comes up with a better way to serve that niche and proceeds to expand like crazy by buying out some smaller competitors and stealing market shares from the rest.

As a consolidator grows, it achieves economies of scale—the ability to produce mass quantities more cheaply and to negotiate lower prices from suppliers on large purchases. This allows it to cut prices and/or raise profits, which further increases its advantage over smaller competitors.

At any given time, dozens of industries are in the process of consolidation. See the sections in the previous chapter on Nashville and Detroit for how it's happening in health care and auto parts, respectively. But entrepreneurs are also trying it in fields as disparate as animal hospitals and seed production.

Open Plan Systems (PLAN) is a good example of an early-stage consolidator. After several successful years as a private company, it went public in 1996 and launched an attempt to consolidate the field of workstation recycling. PLAN takes used workstations, those desk/cubicle combinations consisting of metal frames covered with cloth and metal desks covered with laminate, strips the paint and cloth from them and recovers them so that they're indistinguishable from new. The stations then sell for 30 to 50 percent less than new ones.

Because new offices are constantly being established and old workstations constantly wearing out, there is both a growing supply of raw material, i.e., old workstations, and a strong demand for refurbished ones. And because the field is relatively new, it's full of little guys, most of whom have one factory and very little marketing expertise.

As this is written, Open Plan is experiencing growing pains, and its stock is off its highs. But the obscurity of the field gives it plenty of time to get things right.

QUESTIONS FOR A CONSOLIDATOR. You'll want answers to the following questions when you encounter a consolidator. As always, the two quickest sources of help are a local broker, who either knows the company or has access to an analyst who does, and the company's investor relations people, who should know much of this already and can get at least some of the rest.

- *How big is the overall industry?* Total sales in the United States and, if applicable, worldwide.
- *How fragmented is it?* In other words, how many little guys are out there doing the same thing?
- *How are economies of scale achieved in this particular industry?*
- *How easy has it been—and is it likely to be—for the company to get expansion capital?*
- *Are there other consolidators in this field?* How big are they in relation to your consolidator? How profitable? How do their strategies and business practices differ from those of your consolidator? Where are they geographically? How soon are they likely to run into each other?
- *Are the other consolidators potential acquirers or acquirees of the company you're analyzing?*

The category killer. This company moves into markets where the dominant players feature a wide selection. But instead of also offering variety, it takes one piece of the business and does it better and cheaper than the big, less-well-focused guys.

Category killers have traditionally thrived in retailing. Circuit

City (CC), for instance, has built an empire on its consumer electronics superstore concept—big, clean stores that offer stereos and computers for less than either small local electronics shops or sprawling department stores. Now it's trying to do the same thing in used cars. It recently created and took public CarMax, (KMX) a chain of "used-car superstores," which is applying the wide selection/low price/no haggling framework to a market sorely in need of it.

Another area that looks ripe for category killers is medicine. Think of a hospital as a department store with different areas labeled cancer, heart disease and maternity, and you get a feel for the magnitude of the opportunity. In her book *Market Driven Health Care*, Harvard Business School professor Regina Herzlinger predicts that the future of health care lies in the "focused factory," a kind of mini-hospital that takes one aspect of medicine and does it very, very well: "Focused factories could be established that specialize in any of the millions of high-volume procedures, such as births, cataract surgeries, and bypass operations. . . . General purpose hospitals cannot duplicate the intensity and quality of this attention, because their staff's focus is diffused over a wider range of services."

At least one public company is putting this idea into practice: MedCath (MCTH) is creating a chain of "heart hospitals," which, like Circuit City stealing business from Sears, are designed to dominate heart surgery and related treatments in their target markets. After identifying a metropolitan area with the right demographics—i.e., a lot of old people—MedCath contacts the cream of the local crop of cardiologists and cardiovascular surgeons and asks if they'd be interested in investing in a new, state-of-the-art heart hospital. Most like the idea of owning their own place of business and buy in. Once the hospital is up and running, the doctor/owners then steer their patients to it, filling it almost immediately.

QUESTIONS FOR A CATEGORY KILLER:

- *What advantages does the company have over its diversified competitors?*
- *Have you visited its store/tried its service or product?* Do you know someone who has? What do you/they think?
- *How easy would it be for diversified competitors to blunt this advantage?*
- *Has this been tried in the past? What happened?*
- *Who else is currently trying similar things?*
- *How do the other guys differ from your category killer?*
- *Is the market big enough to accommodate several such category killers?*
- *How soon will their growth paths put them on a collision course?*

The new twist on an old idea. In the annals of pointless behavior, creating a new restaurant chain would seem to rank right up there with telling your friends the truth about their hair or advocating cuts in Social Security.

The business of feeding people has already been partially consolidated, economies of scale are monumental (can you imagine the discount McDonald's gets on beef?) and the minimum wage keeps going up. The same goes for specialty retailing, which is dominated by giants like Home Depot and Circuit City, and consumer products, where Procter and Gamble and its peers spend billions annually on research and advertising.

And yet each year entrepreneurs attack these markets from hundreds of different angles, and a fair number of them win big with ideas that had somehow previously escaped the rest of the industry.

This is possible for two reasons: First, the markets in question are so big that there's always room for a hot new concept, and second, people get bored. We're always looking for something new, different and intriguing, and we're willing to pay a premium for it, even if it's not accompanied by a demonstrable increase in quality or utility. New is valuable, in other words, because in and of itself it produces pleasure.

This kind of company—especially if it deals in food, clothing or some other easily understood field—offers you the chance to do firsthand research, and to judge for yourself whether the new idea has legs.

One new restaurant chain that looks like a textbook case is Logan's Roadhouse (RDHS). Logan's owns thirty casual dining restaurants in Tennessee and surrounding states. Its restaurants are reminiscent of the American roadhouse, with neon lights and murals of the American West on the walls. Inside, customers find vats of free roasted peanuts, and are encouraged to throw the shells on the floor. The menu features moderately priced steaks, ribs, chicken and seafood, as well as signature dishes like fried green tomatoes and baked sweet potatoes.

Sales have tripled since 1993 and current plans call for an acceleration of restaurant building in coming years. Same-store sales aren't rising much, but are stable at a highly profitable level.

The new-twist-on-an-old-idea concept isn't limited to store chains, however. Consep (CSEP), for example, is trying to replace several widely used toxic pesticides with environmentally friendly alternatives. Instead of using poisons to kill bugs, Consep's products use natural pheromones to inhibit their mating. This causes insect populations to plunge to levels at which they are no longer a problem for farmers. "Birth control for bugs," says the company's literature.

Consep's earnings are still minimal, and the past couple of years have been marred by one kind of disappointment or another. But its two newest products are on track to set first-year records for their respective categories. And several trends, including new strains of pesticide-resistant bugs and new findings about the toxicity of some pesticides, point toward rising demand in the future.

QUESTIONS FOR A "NEW TWIST" COMPANY:

- *What's the company's advantage over the existing competitors?*
- *Has it found a way to deliver quality—or the perception of quality—at a reasonable cost? How?*
- *Can it deliver the same value at a lower cost?*
- *Does it have a style that sets it apart?* Pier 1 Imports, for example, has created an atmosphere that causes otherwise normal people to desire wicker furniture. And steak houses are everywhere, but Outback Steakhouse, with its Aussie élan, seems to make people especially carnivorous.
- *How easy would it be for a major competitor to wipe out this advantage by making a relatively minor adjustment, like cutting the price of a given product?* For example: Low-cost burger chains made a splash in the early 1990s, but because their only ad-

vantage was cost, their growth stalled when Burger King halved the price of the Whopper. A decade earlier the major airlines destroyed upstart discount carriers like People Express by simply cutting prices on a small portion of their tickets.

- *Is the appeal regional or can it work nationally?*
- *Does management have a growth plan that's both detailed and reasonable?*

The breakthrough product. This is frequently the hardest type of company to figure out, because breakthroughs often involve a technology that no one outside a tiny circle of Ph.D.'s really grasps. On the other hand, if it works, a lot of people will want to buy it.

Here's an example from medicine, where breakthroughs are a daily occurrence: Gliatech (GLIA) is creating a line of gels designed to inhibit postoperative scarring, a nasty and unpredictable side effect of many kinds of surgery. GLIA just got approval to start marketing one product in the United States. And it's working on a whole series of new gels, each aimed at a specific kind of operation. The potential market is in the hundreds of millions of dollars.

The problem with a company like Gliatech is that unlike, say, a restaurant chain, you have no easy way of judging firsthand whether what they're selling is effective. Furthermore, it's virtually certain that other very smart people are working on similar products, and might at any time release something even better.

Still, Wall Street loves this kind of thing, and if the breakthrough ends up working, the company's early investors get to experience one of the most thrilling rides this side of Disney World.

QUESTIONS FOR A BREAKTHROUGH PRODUCT COMPANY:

- *Does the breakthrough product really, really work?* Are there test results from high-quality sources, testimonials from satisfied users, large orders from highly discriminating customers?
- *What's the competition?* Do ten other major companies have divisions working on the same thing? Or have they tried and abandoned the idea as unworkable?
- *What's the market if it's successful?*

The turnaround. Companies, like people, will occasionally screw up. They'll try something that fails, they'll overextend themselves financially, they'll find numerous ingenious ways to lose money and credibility.

But redemption is possible, and the lessons learned often carry the seeds of future success. Or today's troubles might provide the impetus for sweeping away the old management team and their strategies and bringing in people who have different, better ideas.

The beauty of turnarounds is that when a company stumbles, investors tend to lose interest, and will often take a long, long time to come back. In the process, a huge imbalance can build up between what the company is worth and what the market thinks it's worth. And if it happens nearby, you'll see the changes before anyone else.

Turnaround stories are everywhere. Chrysler was given up for dead as recently as 1990. Its bonds were junk—unattractive junk at that—and most observers expected it to be a division of Honda or Toyota before long.

Instead, it revamped its production methods and brought out a series of innovative new cars, trucks and vans, something that might have been impossible if both managers and unions weren't desperate. The new vehicles were hits, and Chrysler's stock ran from four dollars at its 1990 trough to thirty-six dollars five years later.

IBM is another fascinating story: In the early 1990s the mainframe computer was declared obsolete by industry analysts. And IBM, the king of mainframes, would, they said, be better off broken up into small, agile pieces. Instead, it brought in new management, stuck to its core businesses while slashing costs and came back strong, tripling in market value in three years.

Even Open Plan, our consolidator example, became a potential turnaround after growing pains chased away its early backers. Its stock price fell by about 60 percent, and as of mid-1997 it was trading below book value and at two thirds of sales. Now, in near total obscurity, it's trying to fix what went wrong. If it succeeds, its few remaining shareholders have much to look forward to.

But note that a lot of companies go down and stay down. So before buying a turnaround, you'll want to see tangible signs of success. It makes sense, in fact, to treat a turnaround company much the same way you would an emerging growth situation. First demand an idea that is demonstrably working, then positive trends in operating stats to validate the concept.

QUESTIONS FOR A TURNAROUND CANDIDATE:

- *What caused the original problems?*
- *Is the same crowd who caused the trouble still running things?* If so, what are they doing differently?
- *Is a new management team in place?* If so, what are they doing differently?
- *What have the new managers done that qualifies them to turn this company around?* Are they experts in the industry? Have they built/rescued/run similar companies? Do they have connections to other companies or people who help?
- *Are there tangible signs of a turnaround, such as rising sales, big orders, joint ventures with successful companies or equity investments from other companies in the field?*
- *If the troubles were financial, how much healthier is the balance sheet?* Has debt—especially short-term debt—been reduced? Have new bank credit lines been secured? How much cash is on hand, and how long will it last if current trends continue?

Some General Considerations

Once you understand what a company does, you'll want to investigate the following:

Quality of management. With an emerging company, you're buying three things: a strategy, some early numbers and a management team. And of the three, the last might be the most important.

That's because a business strategy, like the outline of a novel, is just a starting point. Turning it into a viable, growing company is an incredibly complex process. Factories have to be planned and built, then run efficiently. People must be hired, trained and motivated. Markets must be targeted and the right customers cultivated. It's a huge job when you think about it, with countless opportunities to squander that good idea.

Meanwhile, all of the above takes cash. So management has to be able to both make the right decisions and convince bankers and investors to put up the money needed to expand.

For an example of a strong management team at a young company, consider AgriBioTech (ABTX). This is a "seed" company in both senses of the word—a start-up that's attempting to consolidate one of the last remaining fragmented parts of the seed business: alfalfa and other forage grasses, which are used mostly for cattle feed. It spent the years between 1994 and 1997 using other people's money to acquire competing firms in an attempt to build a nationwide seed-distribution capability.

Its top management and their relevant experience:

Chief Executive Officer: Johnny Thomas, Ph.D. Raised on a forage farm and owns alfalfa farms in New Mexico, he's a former director of research for North American Plant Breeders, a division of Royal Dutch Shell, where he supervised all research programs and developed several forage and turf varieties. He has a doctorate in genetics/plant breeding, with a thesis in forage breeding.
Chief Financial Officer: Henry Ingalls, a partner at KPMG Peat Marwick since 1978, where he participated in more than 125 securities offerings, totaling over $5 billion.
Chief of Strategic Planning: Kathleen Gillespie, formerly manager of seed operations for Agway, a major seed distributor.
Vice President/Director: John Francis, a thirty-year veteran in

the cattle industry, with stints running both ranches and feed lots.

Because Thomas and his team are creating AgriBioTech from scratch, they're gobbling capital. Therefore, their ability to raise money is crucial. And so far they've consistently been able to get new lines of credit and sell their stock via both public offerings and private placements. This is certainly not because of AgriBioTech's operating earnings, which didn't exist prior to 1997, and it's probably not because people find the alfalfa business glamorous. Rather, it's because the guys building the company know whereof they speak. Their experience, in short, guarantees that they'll get the chance to test their ideas.

Now consider Omni Multimedia (OMG). Omni is an established company with a decade-long track record in software duplication and fulfillment. That is, it took software originals, copied them onto three-and-a-half-inch floppy disks, packed them up and mailed them off. When CD-ROMs began to supplant floppy disks, Omni was forced to migrate along with the market. It raised $5 million in an IPO and began building a CD-ROM manufacturing plant. Its management:

Chief Executive Officer: Paul Johnson, founder and, since 1980, head of Omni. No experience with CD-ROM manufacturing facilities.

Chief Financial Officer: Robert Lee, formerly CEO of LGM Corp., a $65 million maker of helicopter transmissions and glass-forming machinery. Prior to that he was a consultant to venture capitalists.

Chief Operating Officer: Richard Pilotte, head of operations since Omni's inception. Previously a manager with two packaging companies.

At the time of its 1995 IPO, the CD-ROM market was booming and Omni's migration to this platform appeared to make sense. Before the first CD-ROM line was in place, in fact, Omni announced that demand was so much higher than expected that it was accelerating its expansion. To raise the extra cash it sold about $9 million of convertible preferred stock. At the same time, company management was making specific, very favorable sales and earnings projections for the coming year. Omni's stock reflected this optimism, trading into the low teens in anticipation of the coming CD-ROM boom.

Then the problems began. The CD-ROM line took longer to set up than expected, and the three-and-a-half-inch business collapsed. As a result, not only did Omni's subsequent earnings come in below expectations but its quarterly sales actually declined year-over-year, harsh news indeed for an emerging growth company.

If this were not bad enough, the preferred stock issue turned out to include a clause that let holders convert to common stock at a 15 percent discount to the market, with no minimum price. So, as the stock fell on disappointing earnings, preferred holders began converting to common stock and dumping it, sending its price down to less than one dollar a share, where it languishes as this is written.

Omni's moral? A logical idea failed because it was badly implemented. The fact that no one in top management had done anything like this before might have been a tipoff that trouble was likely. So might have the no-floor-price conversion clause in the preferred issue.

In reality, however, so many things can go wrong that no one can anticipate them all. That's why manager/owners who have been there before are a far better bet than those who are learning as they go along.

Insider transactions. There is probably no better indication of where a company is headed than what the people running it are doing with their stock. If anyone knows what's happening, so goes the theory, it's the people who see the latest sales figures, negotiate with suppliers and spy on competitors.

But selling and buying aren't equally valuable indicators. Since managers of growing companies often have most of their personal wealth tied up in their firm, it's normal and reasonable for them to sell stock to diversify as the company grows, even if they like its prospects. So there is usually a "background noise" level of insider selling that's not correlated with any particular movement in a stock's price. It's only when the selling accelerates that you've got a warning sign.

A good example is Herbalife International (HERB), a former high flier whose stock began falling in January 1997. By April, the stock was down by 50 percent, and bargain hunters were wondering if a bottom was near. Maybe not, concluded a *Wall Street Journal* article at the time: Herbalife's top people had just finished dumping nearly 300,000 shares of stock at the current low; if they don't consider the stock undervalued, then neither, logic dictates, should investors.

Buying, on the other hand, is a more consistently valuable signal, on the assumption that if insiders are already heavily invested in their company and what they're seeing makes them want even more, then what they're seeing must be really exciting.

Consider Octel (OCTL), a maker of cutting-edge voice-mail/E-mail systems. This was a very hot field in the mid-1990s, and Octel's stock was a major winner. But in mid-1996 it missed a product delivery deadline and saw its stock price fall by 50 percent.

However, as it languished in fallen angel purgatory, the insiders were buying the stock aggressively. In the six months prior to January 1997, they bought 483,000 shares. And how they did it was just as notable: They exercised options they had received as part of their compensation packages, then held on to the stock. These options were nonqualified, meaning that the holders incurred a tax liability on the date they bought the stock. Normally, executives who exercise such options immediately sell stock to pay their taxes, and Octel's insiders had a history of doing just that. So the fact that this time they paid cash to exercise the options, then paid cash again to cover their taxes, indicated that they expected to announce good news in the coming year.

Good news was indeed forthcoming. Six months after the article appeared, Octel agreed to be acquired by Lucent (formerly Bell Labs) for a premium of about 50 percent over the price the insiders paid.

To analyze how important a given episode of insider trading is, note how much stock was bought or sold in relation to the shares outstanding, and how broad-based the action is. For example, two officers buying 1,000 shares apiece, when their company has 10 million shares outstanding, isn't much of a signal.

But five officers buying 10,000 shares each is probably worth noting.

Liquidity. One of the great handicaps of emerging growth stocks is a lack of liquidity. This can mean several things, all having to do with how easy (or hard) it is for mutual funds and other big investors to trade large amounts of a company's stock without distorting the price. The harder it is, the fewer institutional money managers, such as mutual funds and pension funds, are able to buy the stock. There are three ways to judge a stock's liquidity:

1. The "float," which is the amount of stock that's free to circulate. To calculate the float, subtract the number of shares held by insiders from the total that's been issued. A small float indicates poor liquidity.
2. Market capitalization (a.k.a. market cap or market value), which is the price times the number of shares outstanding. Companies with market values below $300 million are generally referred to as small-cap, and are considered to be relatively illiquid.
3. Trading volume, which is available from most quote services along with the current price. Many newspapers also list the prior day's volume with each day's quote.
    There's no rule-of-thumb dividing line between liquid and illiquid trading volume, but it's safe to say that an average daily volume of less than 10,000 shares is illiquid in the eyes of major money managers, while better than 100,000 is liquid.

The dilemma for an emerging company is how to get that added liquidity that makes it acceptable to big investors. Just issuing new shares when your stock is already depressed is something managers—generally the largest existing stockholders—are reluctant to do. And splitting the stock when it's already at, say, eight dollars, risks driving it down into penny-stock territory, where institutions will find other reasons for not being interested.

Often, there is no easy answer, and as a result some companies do good things financially and operationally for a long time before they achieve enough liquidity to attract Wall Street's attention. But when they do, look out.

This happened to Pomeroy Computer Resources (PMRY), a computer services company based in Erlanger, Kentucky, that had the bright idea of using its local connections to appeal to local organizations such as state and city government agencies and regional companies. It worked beautifully, and Pomeroy grew dramatically in the early and mid-1990s.

But because Kentucky is so far from the headquarters of most money managers, hardly anyone seemed to care. Pomeroy had attracted some favorable coverage from Roney & Co., a Detroit-based brokerage house. Closer to home, Cincinnati-based Glazer Capital was doing background reports on it, but not making recommendations. That was it, despite the extraordinary numbers.

I called the Glazer analyst for his opinion in early 1996, and he allowed that, yes, Pomeroy was indeed a great company, but that it was too illiquid for his firm's institutional clients.

But Pomeroy needed expansion capital, so later that year, even though its price was undervalued by just about any measure, it decided to sell a million shares of stock. Just as you'd expect, this had the initial effect of knocking the price down a bit. Pomeroy sold the stock anyhow, raising its float to a still minuscule 3 million shares.

Then things started happening. Its next quarterly report was a blowout, with triple-digit growth in both sales and earnings. This combination of fast earnings growth and more shares in circulation seemed, at long last, to pique the interest of a few money managers, who bid the stock up to the mid-twenties. Pomeroy seized this opportunity to declare a three-for-two stock split, increasing the float by another 50 percent.

The stock then went on a second run, peaking at triple its level of a year before.

Table 7.1
POMEROY'S NUMBERS

	1996	1995*	1994*	1993*
Revenues ($ mil.)	336.4	211.1	130.3	102.4
Net income ($ mil.)	6.2	4.4	2.7	1.9
Earnings per share ($)	1.15	1.62	1.12	0.78
Shares outstanding (000s)	5,391	2,659	2,429	2,433
Year-end price ($)	36	15	11	11
Market cap ($ mil.)	194	40	28	26
Price/earnings ratio	31	9	10	14

*Figures for 1995, 1994 and 1993 are as reported, not adjusted for subsequent splits.

The lesson: Illiquidity can be your friend, because it tends to make emerging companies cheap—not in all cases at all times, but frequently enough to produce the occasional Pomeroy. This gives you a chance to get in early and then watch as the virtuous cycle of rising earnings/expanding liquidity/higher stock price works to your advantage.

Customers. A strong relationship with one or two big customers can be an extraordinary blessing to a small company if it means steady, large orders that allow it to get established.

It can also be a serious risk, because the relationship could sour, taking a sizable chunk of the company's business with it. Small companies face that dilemma constantly. To satisfy the demands that, say, Sears makes for a given product, a small supplier might have to buy a massive amount of equipment and inventory and then hire and train a lot of people. This pays off if the relationship holds, and threatens the small company's existence if it doesn't.

An example: ITI Corp. (ITII) makes the newest generation of wireless home-security systems. Until 1997 it was growing quickly thanks to a good relationship with ADT, the largest installer of such systems. But then ADT ended the relationship, leaving ITI with a lot of quiet factory space. Its stock plunged in response, to about half its previous high.

Obviously, other things being equal, a diversified customer base is a major plus. And if a company is dependent on one large customer (or supplier, for that matter), it should have a reasonable plan for weaning itself away from that dependence, without antagonizing its patron. Customer information can be found in the 10-K report, and is often footnoted in the annual report.

New orders. Companies will often announce that they've received a big new order for whatever it is they sell, and this announcement will appear long before the order has an impact on published financial information. That gives you an early line on a trend change, in sales at least.

The key is to understand how big and how firm the new order is, and what it implies about future orders. For example, consider Aetrium (ATRM), a small maker of microchip manufacturing equipment. In 1996, the chip market plateaued and orders plunged for Aetrium's machines. So did Aetrium's stock. Then, in early 1997, the company announced that it had received orders for its new generation of equipment totaling $17 million.

Now, $17 million is a pittance for the average big company. But Aetrium's overall sales were around $40 million in 1996, so the new orders appear to guarantee that 1997 will be a good year. It also implies either that the market for semiconductor equipment is coming back or that the new product is a major advance, or both. Either way, it's a piece of good news that people watching only earnings reports won't see for a while.

Now, for (Just a Few) Numbers

Once you've decided that a company has the basics—a promising strategy and a management team with the experience to carry it off—it's time to put a value on its stock. Because the techniques of stock valuation are so widely available, I won't rehash the definitions of P/E ratios or profit margins here. But with the emerging companies you're turning up, there is one valuation measure that deserves mention: sales.

In standard security analysis, sales (otherwise known as revenue or "the top line") gets less attention than things like earnings, book value and dividend yield.

But since many of the local companies you'll discover are "development stage," which is a nice way of saying that they haven't yet proved that they're capable of turning a sustainable, measurable profit, their sales might be the only hard number you have to go on.

To hear what this number has to say, first calculate its rate of growth, as expressed in percentage terms over the prior year or prior quarter. If March quarter revenues are $10 million, the immediately preceding quarter $7 million, and the previous year's March quarter $5 million, then you've got year-over-year growth of 100 percent ($10 million / $5 million) and sequential growth of 43 percent ($10 million / $7 million). The year-over-year number is usually considered to be a more reliable gauge of how a company is doing because it eliminates seasonal variations.

There are no rules for how fast sales should be growing. Generally speaking, you're looking for rapid growth during the early stages of a company's life. This is the single clearest indication of the validity of a company's strategy—that customers are willing to spend increasing amounts of money on whatever it is the company is selling.

Sales as a valuation measure. To arrive at a rough value for a company's stock, divide the stock price by annual sales per share (or sales into market cap). This is the price/sales ratio, and it tells you how much you're paying for each dollar of a company's sales. Once calculated, it can then be compared with other companies in the same business for a measure of how reasonably your company's stock is priced.

Here's how you might approach AgriBioTech, which you may recall from the discussion of management a few pages back. It was still generating start-up losses in 1996, and the jury was out on whether the venture would succeed. But it did have revenues, allowing a comparison with the field's established players.

Compared with the other seed companies, AgriBioTech was growing faster, was not yet profitable and—because of its obscurity and its losses—was trading at a much lower multiple of sales. The conclusion: If it succeeds in turning its acquisitions into a functioning, profitable company, and is accorded a valuation at the low end of the industry norm, its market value will rise dramatically.

Table 7.2
AGRIBIOTECH COMPARED TO OTHER SEED
COMPANIES

Company	Stock price 5/28/96	Market cap ($ mil.)	Market cap/revenue 1996	1997 est.	P/E multiple 1997 est.	Price/ book value
Pioneer	$54.50	4,523	2.7	2.5	19.5	5.1
DeKalb	$29.00	493	1.6	1.5	28.1	5.2
Mycogen	$17.75	541	3.8	3.1	59.2	3.6
Delta Pine	$45.00	868	4.1	3.1	38.5	22.4
AgriBioTech	$ 3.75	29	1.0	0.3	12.5	2.1

Source: Liviakis Financial Communications, Inc.

Tax loss carryforwards. Another feature of emerging companies is that they tend to run up some serious losses in the course of emerging. And as a result, tucked away on their balance sheet is a hidden asset called tax loss carryforwards (TLCs), that they can use to wipe out future tax liabilities. TLCs are often overlooked by standard security analysis because established companies seldom have them. But for emerging companies, they can be a source of extra cash for years to come.

For More on Security Analysis

This chapter's use of sales as a valuation measure can be adapted to any measure of profitability. Simply substitute a company's net earnings or gross profit for sales and compare it to the major players in the company's field.

As for deciding what's valid in a given situation, that takes us into the realm of mainstream security analysis. There are dozens of books on the subject, but two sources stand out, combining simplicity with legitimacy. One, of course, is Lynch's *One Up on Wall Street*, about which enough has already been said. The other is just about anything on or by Warren Buffett.

Buffett is a once-in-a-lifetime phenomenon, on several levels. Now one of the richest men on the planet, he's the only one in that select group to get there from scratch via the stock market. The rest either inherited their money or made it by starting a company and riding its value upward. He has also apparently avoided the delusions of grandeur that most of us would suffer after turning a few hundred dollars into $15 billion. He lives, as he always has, in Omaha, Nebraska, to all outward appearances a normal, slightly nerdy midwestern businessman. And yet his investment style and its results have made him a legend.

Buffett has yet to write a book, but the annual reports of his investment firm, Berkshire Hathaway, are among the world's most eagerly anticipated and widely read pieces of financial reporting. Written in plain English, they combine wit and modesty with a preternatural insight into the nuts and bolts of investing.

Several books have been written about Buffett, all of which draw on Berkshire Hathaway's annuals. Read just about any of these, and you can't help but benefit from Buffett's insights on the relative merits of earnings, cash flow, management quality and margins of safety (and on life in general).

Some of it is quantitative, yes, but the math is mostly straight-forward addition and division, and it exists to serve common sense and understanding. A list of sources on both Lynch and Buffett can be found on pages 283–285.

8

SELLING:
WHEN THE STORY'S OVER

A Shakespearean actor of some renown was on his deathbed, surrounded by admirers. One of them, perhaps trying to lighten the mood, complimented him on his performance in this, his most difficult role.

"No," he replied with a weak but dismissive wave of his hand. "Dying is easy. *Comedy* is hard."

The investment world has a similar sentiment: Buying is easy, selling is hard.

When you buy stock, there are basically three possible outcomes—win, lose or draw—only one of which causes emotional distress. But once you start contemplating getting out, you're exposed to variations of at least four nasty scenarios:

1. The round trip, where the stock goes up but you get greedy, don't take your profits, and watch helplessly as it falls back to the purchase price, wiping out the paper fortune that you've spent so much time counting and mentally (hopefully only mentally) spending.

2. The premature bailout, where you take what seems like a reasonable profit only to see the stock keep going up, leaving you on the sidelines, impotently calculating what you could have made if you'd only kept the courage of your convictions.

3. The panic bailout, when a stock falls and you cut your losses only to see it turn around and go through the roof.

4. The long ride to oblivion, where a stock goes down and you consider selling but figure why bother, it can't go any lower. But it does, drifting irregularly downward until it becomes a piece of portfolio detritus, worth less than the commission required to sell it, and just sits there ever after, mocking your bad judgment and indecisiveness.

As you can tell, I've seen a few of these. And unfortunately, you won't find a foolproof formula here for avoiding such occurrences. The future is unknowable, and you will never catch every high and low. You can, however, rationalize the process of deciding when to sell.

Let's start with the proposition that your real goal is not to sell. Warren Buffett, for instance, attributes much of his success to the "permanent" investments he's made in a handful of companies, like Coca-Cola and *The Washington Post*. All have traded down temporarily, and all have at times been overvalued by conventional measures. But because Buffett understood why his favorite companies were succeeding, and had faith in their strategies, management and products—their stories, if you will—he held on through the fluctuations, and in the end made himself and his backers a fortune.

The lesson? As long as a company's story is intact, what

the market thinks of its stock is not very important. Put another way, the key to selling is to understand as clearly as possible why you bought the stock in the first place. Only when this changes in some fundamental way is it necessary to re-evaluate.

To visualize this process, let's consider Wal-Mart. Here's how an investor in the 1980s might have composed its story:

> Wal-Mart is a chain of variety superstores, selling just about anything you can imagine at low prices. It sets up on the outskirts of small-to-medium-sized towns and takes business from downtown mom-and-pop retailers. Same-store sales are growing at 10 percent or better, margins are stable at a highly profitable level, return on equity exceeds 30 percent and new stores are being added aggressively.

Chart 8.1 shows Wal-Mart's stock price bordered by two lines, one representing a P/E ratio of approximately 20, the other a P/E of 30. Notice that the stock pierced the upper end of its range in 1987, and for a while thereafter underperformed the market. Had you sold at this point of apparent over-valuation, you would, for a year or so, have had reason to gloat. But eventually you would have found yourself on the sidelines, lamenting the easy money you had passed up.

Had you, on the other hand, focused on the story, which was unchanged from 1970 to the early 1990s, you might have ignored the market and held on.

But in early 1993, the ride came to an end. Wal-Mart's stock

Chart 8.1 WAL-MART

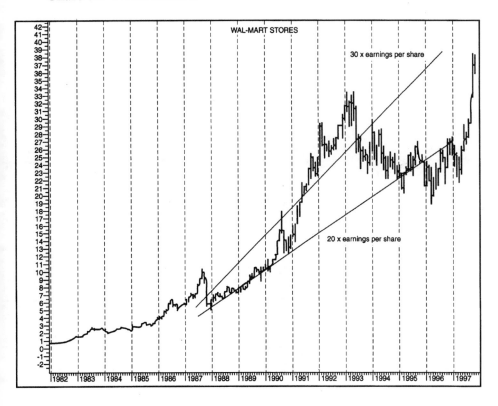

plateaued, then dipped, and then treaded water for the next four years. To see why, turn to Wal-Mart's numbers (table 8.1). You'll notice that overall sales continued to rise right through fiscal 1997, while gross margins stayed in their normal range of 20 to 21 percent.

But return on equity and return on assets had both peaked in the early 1990s, and were in long-term decline. And growth in same-store sales, a measure of how well existing stores are doing, fell off the table in 1994, dropping to 6 percent, the first time since 1986 that the figure had been below 10 percent.

Table 8.1
WAL-MART'S NUMBERS

	1996	1995	1994	1993	1992	1991	1990	1989
Net sales ($ mil.)	93,627	82,494	67,344	55,484	43,887	32,602	25,811	20,649
% change	13	22	21	26	35	26	25	29
Gross profit ($ mil.)	19.0	16.9	13.9	11.5	9.1	7.1	5.7	4.6
Gross margin %	20.4	20.5	20.7	20.7	20.9	21.8	22.0	22.3
Inventory turnover	17.0	17.1	16.3	16.8	16.9	17.8	17.0	16.5
Earnings per share ($)	1.19	1.17	1.02	0.87	0.70	0.57	0.48	0.37
% change	2	15	17	24	23	19	30	32
Same-store sales (% change)	4	7	6	11	10	10	11	12

Source: Wal-Mart's 1996 annual report

The shrinking margins and decelerating same-store sales growth—which, based on the stock's action, probably became apparent in 1993's second quarter—were important clues that something had changed. And in retrospect, something had: K mart and Sears were finally getting their acts together, and new, specialized competitors like Circuit City and Home Depot were eating into Wal-Mart's franchise in consumer electronics and hardware. Wal-Mart, in short, was no longer invincible. Its aggressive investment in new stores was no longer generating the same high returns.

Yet, during this time, you could have visited your local Wal-Mart and seen a crowded parking lot, just like always. Its overall sales continued to surge. And many people continued to buy and hold the stock on the assumption that the world's greatest retail chain would come back, just as it always had. But it didn't, at least not for a long time. By the end of 1996, its price was below its 1993 peak, while the overall market had doubled.

Overvaluation

The fact that price matters less than the strength of the story does not mean that price never matters. Sometimes, for instance, the market may be so excited by a company's prospects that it pushes the stock's price far beyond its normal range, making a big pullback inevitable. Because you're working with a limited amount of capital, you may have to sell one position in order to take another. In that case, you'll want to know which of your stocks are over- and undervalued. This requires that you establish some guidelines in the form of a trading range based on the stock's past relationship to some relevant financial indicator.

The idea that a stock can be charted against its long-term cash flow, giving an investor a quick snapshot of its value relative to its history, is one of the seminal ideas of *The Value Line Investment Survey* (the source of the newsletter's name, in fact). But you can also use P/E (as with Wal-Mart a few pages back), Price/Sales, Price/Book and dividend yield. Deciding which is most relevant and setting up a chart to visualize it can be a bit of a chore with paper, pencil and calculator, but it's well worth the trouble. And with one of the better investment software programs (see chapter 10), it's a snap.

Once a range is established, note when it's pierced. If the breakout is on the low side and the story hasn't changed, that's a possible buy signal. On the high side, it denotes a potential source of cash.

The Tax Consequences of Selling

My grandmother-in-law is living proof of the power of compound interest. In her ninety-seven years of modeling, teaching school and caring for her family, she has never earned a great deal of money. And she's lived, without exception, modestly. But in her fifties she developed an interest in the stock market and began buying tiny bits of companies that intrigued her. Then she put them away and went back to doting on her granddaughter and tending her garden.

Some of these companies have survived, and grown. And

grown. Over the course of decades she's accumulated a portfolio of stocks that originally cost a few hundred dollars and are now worth orders of magnitude more. She's also accumulated something else: a massive unrealized capital gain. Today, despite a continuing interest in the market, she's frozen in place, because to buy something she'll have to sell something else. And that means paying the government an unacceptably large part of her estate.

Which leads us to the last piece of the when-to-sell puzzle: calculating how much the IRS will skim off the top, and factoring this into your alternative uses for the money.

Let's say one of your stocks has doubled. That means half of the sale price is profit, taxable at capital gains rates. If your tax bracket is 20 percent, you lose 10 percent (20 percent times the half of the sale price that is profit) of your proceeds. So, to make this guaranteed immediate reduction in your net worth a good idea, the stock's overvaluation—or the alternative stock's undervaluation—must be that much more extreme.

Shorting: Sell High, Buy Low

If you're the adventurous type, and very sure of a stock's overvaluation, there's a way to turn this certainty into cash. It's called selling short, or shorting, and it works like this: You tell your broker to short XYZ Corp. He goes out and borrows the stock from the account of someone who owns it, then sells it and deposits the proceeds in your account.

Now you are "short" XYZ, meaning that you profit when it

falls and lose when it rises. Once it drops to a more reasonable level, just as you knew it would, you buy it back to close out the short position (known as "covering"). Your profit is the difference between what you got for selling and what you spent to close the position.

Note that with shorting, your risk is the upside potential of the stock you've sold. In other words, your profit is capped at 100 percent, if the stock goes to zero. But your loss potential (the stock's upside) is theoretically unlimited. So, before you decide to go short, understand that story, and be very sure that it hasn't changed in some extremely favorable way.

Selling Doesn't Mean Saying Good-bye

And now, finally, let's say you've discovered a stock and put in the effort to understand it. You bought it, watched it rise to the point of serious overvaluation and then sold it for a nice profit. Do you forget about it? Absolutely not. Stocks, especially emerging growth stocks, are so volatile that today's overpriced short-sale candidate can become next month's screaming buy, without a change in the basic story.

Here's one—Brightpoint (chart 8.2), which I bought and then sold for what seemed like a decent profit. And because I was busy with other things, this book among them, I stopped paying attention. By the time I came back for another look, it had fallen back to "cheap" territory, then turned around and begun another run.

Had I been paying attention, it would have been easy to verify that the story was still intact (it had, in fact, gotten even better)

Chart 8.2 A MISSED OPPORTUNITY: BRIGHTPOINT

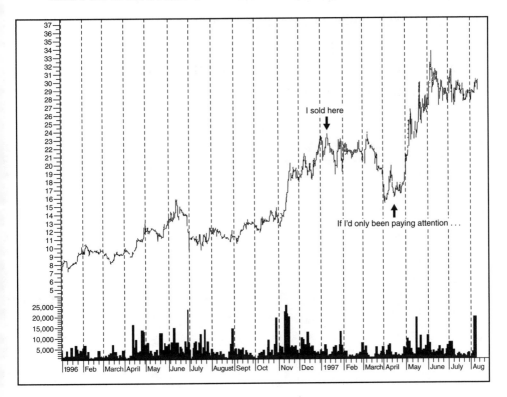

and to jump right back in near the bottom. But because I'd said good-bye after Brightpoint's first run-up, I missed a chance to convert the effort I'd put into learning about it into another nice profit.

The moral? Keep tracking the companies you've gotten to know, even if you no longer own them. Because even after you've taken out your money, you have an investment of time and thought that might yet pay off. If a company's story has changed in an unfavorable way, then it might one day evolve into a turnaround candidate. If the price is too rich, then watch for pullbacks while keeping up with its story.

Companies, in short, are like friends. They can pass out of and then back into your life, making the effort of getting to know them doubly valuable.

9

MAIN STREET IN
CYBERSPACE

Intermediaries are an endangered species. The information
standard has knocked them out. All the world's financial data
is now on-line.
—Walter Wriston, former head of Citibank,
in *Wired* magazine

Think of it as one of life's little ironies. The Internet, by col-
lapsing time and distance and bringing the world to your desktop, has also made it much easier to follow companies that
operate right down the street. With a computer, a modem and
a little patience, you can now monitor local company financial
reports and press releases, get real-time stock quotes and cor-
respond in a zero-stress way with investor relations departments,
local business journal reporters and local brokerage house analysts. You can also track pending and recent IPOs, monitor several different portfolios and even trade stocks for far less money
than traditional brokers charge. All without leaving your most
comfortable chair.

Web surfing, like stock picking, is the subject of a whole spectrum of books. So rather than repeat the basics that are already out there in so many forms, this chapter will assume that you already have a working knowledge of Web browsers, search engines and the like and will go straight to the on-line resources that are most useful for tapping into the local information flow.

Local company Web sites. A Web site is one of those things, like a nice headquarters building and a glossy annual report, that may or may not contribute to the bottom line, but that's just too cool for most companies to resist. So even small firms that don't actually sell products on-line are setting up sites.

Here they paint their self-portrait: Product information, corporate mission statement, recent financials, management profiles, press releases, even analyst reports. All the stuff, in other words, that you might spend weeks putting together is right there, accessible with the touch of your keyboard. Most company sites also allow you to E-mail management.

So take a list of the local companies you'd like to follow, and pull up your favorite search engine. Then begin typing in their names (one search tip: Always surround company names with quotation marks; that way you'll get only sites in which the whole name is prominent). If you've already decided that a company is worth following, call up the site and save it (also known as bookmarking), so that you can return to it for later reference. If you're still deciding, spend some time with the site, checking out recent earnings, perusing management's comments, looking for analyst's reports. If you're feeling ambitious, read the company's product information for suppliers and customers who might have insights into the products' success. Then E-mail the

AN EMERGING COMPANY'S WEB SITE

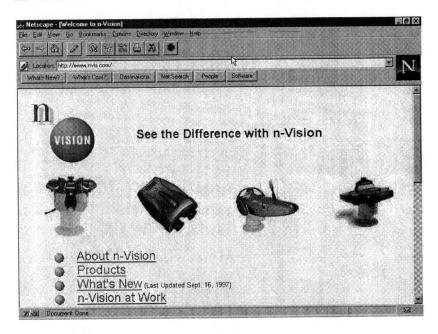

company with a request for an investor's information packet or with specific (and short) questions that occur to you. If the site lists and/or links to analysts who cover the company, you may want to follow those links and see what the analysts think, and then ask a question or two of them.

Once you've saved your companies' sites, go back to them periodically for updates. This alone will keep you better informed than 90 percent of their other investors.

Local business journal sites. The Web, with its magazine-like format, is a natural second home for just about any publication, including local business journals. Despite some concern about the utility of putting geography-specific information on a global medium, they're piling in.

On-line business journals have one huge advantage over their hard-copy brethren: Because of their ability to archive information from back issues, these sites make past data immediately accessible. The best sites already include search engines that allow you to enter the name of a local company and pull up all the feature articles written about it in the recent past. In time, that search function will almost certainly be expanded to include all mentions—earnings reports, press releases and stock-price data—of a given company for as far back as the on-line archives go.

American City Business Journals, a chain of several dozen journals in major cities around the country, seems to be blazing the on-line trail. Each of its journals' sites have the same clear format, including a strong search engine that lets you browse past issues for articles on companies or subjects. And the American City corporate site has a search engine that accesses back issues of all the company's journals.

Some other features of good business journal sites include listings of local experts in various fields. *Business New Jersey*, for instance, offers "Business Experts Online," which connects visitors via E-mail to local experts in various fields. And *Virginia Business* is setting up a database that contains financial information on all Virginia public companies, along with links to their Web sites.

Last but not least, the ability to E-mail a local business journal's reporters is a huge improvement over calling them. Because their job is to be either on the phone with sources or on the road interviewing them, reporters are, by definition, hard to reach. But with E-mail, you send them the message and they answer at their convenience.

Local brokers. If the Web is slightly problematic for local business journals, it's downright threatening for local broker-age houses. Their research is proprietary—that is, they give it to clients in return for the clients trading with them. So post-ing it on the Internet is a little like Ford handing out free Mustangs.

But a few regional brokers are setting up sites, and these, even in their early incarnations, are extraordinarily useful sources of information. At the site of Morgan Keegan, a Memphis-based regional, a visitor can peruse the firm's history and philosophy and get an overview of its capabilities (see illustration on page 162). You'll also find a list of recommended stocks and the lo-cation and telephone numbers of its brokers. Sites like this al-most completely automate the process of finding a local broker. Just check the recommended list to see if it includes emerging companies in your area, E-mail a few brokers in the nearest office and await their replies.

City and regional sites. Cities, states and regions are going on-line, either on their own or via services like CitySearch, Mi-crosoft Sidewalk or America Online's Digital Cities. But so far they seem to be doing it with shoppers and tourists rather than investors in mind. This will change, as participants start looking for ways to differentiate themselves and add some value. Over time, your city's—or the chamber of commerce's—site will be-come more and more useful as a source of ideas. So be aware of it, keep going back to check on its progress and don't hesitate to E-mail them with requests for information on emerging com-panies and other investment-related data. In the meantime, these sites are great for finding new restaurants.

A REGIONAL BROKERAGE HOUSE WEB SITE

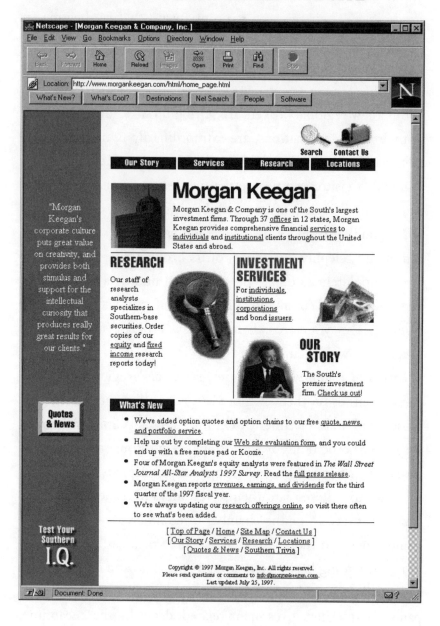

Netscape - [Morgan Keegan & Company, Inc.]

File Edit View Go Bookmarks Options Directory Window Help

Back Forward Home Reload Images Open Print Find Stop

Location: http://www.morgankeegan.com/html/home_page.html

What's New? What's Cool? Destinations Net Search People Software

Search   Contact Us

Our Story | **Services** | **Research** | **Locations**

"Morgan Keegan's corporate culture puts great value on creativity, and provides both stimulus and support for the intellectual curiosity that produces really great results for our clients."

Morgan Keegan

Morgan Keegan & Company is one of the South's largest investment firms. Through 37 offices in 12 states, Morgan Keegan provides comprehensive financial services to individuals and institutional clients throughout the United States and abroad.

RESEARCH

Our staff of research analysts specializes in Southern-base securities. Order copies of our equity and fixed income research reports today!

INVESTMENT SERVICES

For individuals, institutions, corporations and bond issuers.

OUR STORY

The South's premier investment firm. Check us out!

Quotes & News

What's New

- We've added option quotes and option chains to our free quote, news, and portfolio service.
- Help us out by completing our Web site evaluation form, and you could end up with a free mouse pad or Koozie.
- Four of Morgan Keegan's equity analysts were featured in *The Wall Street Journal All-Star Analysts 1997 Survey*. Read the full press release.
- Morgan Keegan reports revenues, earnings, and dividends for the third quarter of the 1997 fiscal year.
- We're always updating our research offerings online, so visit there often to see what's been added.

Test Your Southern I.Q.

[Top of Page / Home / Site Map / Contact Us]
[Our Story / Services / Research / Locations]
[Quotes & News / Southern Trivia]

Document: Done

Specialized local sites. A few farsighted entrepreneurs are setting up sites dedicated solely to their cities' investment communities. For example, San Diego CEO Talk is run by a local public relations firm to give local companies an on-line forum. Companies pay to be included, and investors are invited to visit for free.

Other On-line Resources

Once you've found and saved the Web sites that relate directly to local companies, you'll want some general sources of price quotes, charts, market data and other similar things. The Web, of course, has such things in abundance. Here's an overview of the sites that I either use or would use if I had the time. It is by no means exhaustive, and will probably be obsolete in a few years. But the length of the list gives you an idea of how huge a resource cyberspace has become.

Comprehensive sites. These are sites that try to be all things to an investor, offering price quotes, charting services, news and links to on-line brokers and massive numbers of other sources. The most heavily trafficked finance site is probably America On-line's. I use it, and am more familiar with it than any other. So, for a standard against which to judge the other sites, let's take a look at what you'll find with AOL:

PORTFOLIOS. This function allows you to set up multiple portfolios, which are updated with a fifteen-minute delay from real-time trading. I monitor three—one with stocks I own, another with stocks I'm watching but haven't yet bought and a third with big names that are simply fun to follow.

STOCK REPORTS AND FINANCIAL STATEMENTS. Drawn from

Morningstar and Disclosure, these are overviews of a given company's business and its finances. They make a good starting point for deciding whether to look further.

EARNINGS ESTIMATES. This service taps the First Call database, which tracks the earnings estimates brokerage houses publish for the companies they cover. It gives you three important pieces of information: how many analysts are publishing earnings reports on a given company, what they expect it to earn in the coming year and how often and in what direction they've been revising their estimates.

HISTORICAL PRICES. Here you can generate basic price charts and customize them in a limited way by changing the time frame and adding trading volume and relative strength lines.

EDGAR 10(K)S AND 10(Q)S. Edgar is a Securities and Exchange Commission database that includes most companies' financial reports. Here, you'll find just about everything a company is required to publish, including footnotes, where all the skeletons are buried.

NEWS BY TICKER. Stories and or/press releases on a given company. The database goes back only one month, which is a problem, but it's still invaluable for keeping up with new events in the life of emerging local companies.

THE MOTLEY FOOL (http://www.fool.com) started out as an AOL site dedicated to educating investors and giving them a place to share ideas. But its rising popularity has given it a life of its own. The guiding philosophy of this site is firmly "invest in what you know." Not surprisingly, it includes lots of cogent criticism of Wall Street, like the following:

Just about everyone who you might pay to manage your money underperforms the market—a contingent that includes most full-service brokers and money managers. So how do they keep their clients? By having you believe that they are WISE, and that you, poor Fool, can't possibly make a dollar in the big, scary market without them. Well, we've got news for you. The market ain't that scary and you don't need their Wisdom. . . . Believe it or not, you may have the upper hand.

The Fool is a great place for beginners, and a good place to look for other people with insight into the stocks you're following.

AAII. The American Association of Individual Investors maintains a site on AOL that offers access to that big investor group's background material and software. This is a fairly complete investment site all by itself.

Other comprehensive sites. The following sites offer most of the same features as AOL, but are available on the World Wide Web. Some are free, but many charge monthly or annual fees. An afternoon spent going through this list will be time well spent:

A Trader's Financial Resource Guide (http://www.stocks.com)
Briefing.com (http://www.briefing.com)
DBC Online (http://www.dbc.com)
Interactive Nestegg (http://nestegg.iddis.com)
Investor Insight (http://www.investorinsight.com)
Investors Edge (http://www.irnet.com)
Investors' Square (http://www.investorsquare.com)
Market Guide (http://www.marketguide.com)

Microsoft Investor (http://investor.msn.com)
Money Online (http://www.money.com)
Net Worth (http://www.quotes.galt.com)
PAWWS Financial Network (http://www.pawws.com)
Quote.com (http://www.quote.com)
Zacks Investors Services (http://www.zacks.com)

Specialized sites. The following sites focus on a specific area of investing that might be useful:

IPO Data Systems (http://www.ipodata.com). Lots of background on recent IPOs, along with a fairly sophisticated search engine that allows visitors to sort companies by geography and business type.

IPO Monitor (http://www.ipomonitor.com). This site tracks all the companies that have gone or are planning to go public, gives you the name of the underwriter and the size, date and price of the IPO, and lets you know how the stock has performed since issuance.

Imspectus (http://www.imspectus.com). Allows you to download full prospectuses for current IPOs. The format requires Adobe Acrobat software, which can be downloaded free of charge from this site. The electronic prospectuses are hot-linked, meaning that by clicking one piece of highlighted text, you move immediately to whatever the section is linked with.

Edgar (http://www.edgar-online.com). The SEC's database of 10-Ks, 10-Qs and other company documents.

National Association of Investors Corp. (http://www.better-investing.org). NAIC is the largest sponsor of investment clubs, and its site offers a nice variety of resources for beginning investors and club members. Its Computer Group, for instance, is an on-line forum dedicated to helping members get the most from their investment software. The NAIC is one of the two or three most useful resources you'll find in this book.

STB Investor Software (http://www.stbinvestorsoftware.com). A software development company specializing in investment products, including souped-up versions of NAIC's programs.

American Association of Individual Investors (http://www.networth.galt.com/www/home/planning/aaii/home.html). The AAII is a large organization dedicated to helping people learn about the market. Lots of good common-sense ideas and resources, most aimed at the fairly sophisticated investor.

Investor Relations Information Network (http://www.irin.com). IRIN offers company annual reports, quarterlies, fact books and press releases in their original format. It's free.

Yahoo Quotes (http://www.quote.yahoo.com). From Yahoo, the granddaddy of Internet search engines, this site offers free quotes, news and constantly updated links to other useful financial sites.

The NASDAQ (http://www.nasdaq.com). The emerging stock market's site. A good quote and graph service, with a constantly expanding list of other features.

Pointcast Network (http://www.pointcast.com). A Web-based news service that dials up your Internet connection at regular intervals throughout the day and downloads free on-line news and information directly to your computer screen. It's customizable, meaning that you tell it what subjects are of interest, and it gets them for you. It is said to be very easy to install, and so far is a huge hit with early adopters. As one review puts it, "Your concept of a screen saver will never be the same."

WiseWire (http://www.wisewire.com). A free, customizable news service.

CDA/Investnet (http://www.cda.com/investnet/chronicle/trial.html). The leading source of insider-trading stats.

The American Venture Capital Exchange (http://www.avce.com). Lists more than 250 start-up and expanding companies seeking financing.

CitySearch (http://www.citysearch.com). A service that builds comprehensive city sites, focusing mainly on culture, but with increasing attention to public companies.

Microsoft Sidewalk (http://www.sidewalk.com). Microsoft's city listings.

Site Lists

Since the Web is constantly changing, it's comforting to know that there are people out there at least trying to keep track of it all. The following site lists are worth frequenting:

StockGuys (http://www2.vcn.com/stock/STOCKS.HTM).

ifBG Gottingen Market Place and Quotations (http://www.
wiso.gwdg.de/ifbg/stock1.htm).

The Web Word Guide to Finance (http://www.euro.net/
innovation/Web_Word_Base/TWW1-html/FinTOC1.html).

Bob Gabele's CDA/Investnet hot links (http://www.cda.com/
investnet/other/links.html).

On-line Brokers

A relationship with a local brokerage house is a key part of finding
and following local stocks. But that doesn't mean you have to do
all your trading through them. On-line brokers are easy to use
and frighteningly cheap. Some trades that might run two or three
hundred dollars at a full-service broker will cost about 90 percent
less on-line. My original idea was to present a listing of the major
on-line brokers. But since they're all going on-line, it probably
makes more sense simply to advise you to do an Internet search
for "on-line brokers" when the time comes.

On-line Special Interest Groups

Most cities have on-line groups, variously known as forums, bulletin boards (BBS) or Special Interest Groups (SIGs), in which
like-minded people log on and discuss their passion. The vast
majority of these focus on sex and cars. Some, however, focus
on investing.

Many local AAII chapters, for instance, have special-interest groups that focus on computerized investing. The organization's *Computerized Investing* newsletter lists these groups, along with their activities, in each issue.

The AAII itself operates a BBS that can be reached by computer at (312) 280-8565. There is no cost to use this system beyond any standard telephone charges incurred.

The Joy of E-mail

One of this chapter's recurring themes is the ease with which you can reach companies' brokers and reporters via E-mail. So, instead of explaining how it works with each one, let's examine E-mail here.

This is by far the most frequently used feature of the Internet, with good reason. It's an extraordinarily easy way to keep in touch with people. You type your note and send it, the recipient gets it when it's convenient for him to check his messages, and he responds when he feels like it. No worries about calling at a bad time, no fear of being unable to articulate a complex question. In short, it's a great way to exchange information with local sources about local companies.

Here are examples of messages you might use to generate information on a given company:

To a local business journal reporter:
Dear Ms. Smith,

I enjoyed your April 12 article on XYZ Corp., and would like to learn more about it as a possible investment.

In the course of researching the article, did you speak to anyone who struck you as especially knowledgeable about the company and its prospects? If so, and if you think he might be open to a couple of questions, would you mind responding with his name and, if you have it, his telephone number or E-mail address?

Thanks in advance for the consideration,
John Rubino

To your local broker:
Ray,

Do you know anything about XYZ Corp. (ticker XYZC)? It's headquartered downtown and went public last month. It looks like it might be of interest to your telecommunications analyst.

The *Business Journal* did a story on them last week, which I'll fax to you later today.

When you get a chance, could you have a look and let me know what you think?

Thanks,
John

To a local company's investor relations person:
Dear Mr. Wilson,

I'm a Richmond resident who is considering buying your stock. I called your department last week for an investor's

172 / MAIN STREET, NOT WALL STREET

packet, which arrived yesterday. After looking over the material, I have a few questions:

- What's the early response to your new widget? At the current rate, what level of sales do you expect it to generate? How profitable is it compared to your other products?
- Who do you consider your main competitors? Their names and/or stock tickers will be fine.
- Are any brokerage house analysts—local or otherwise—visiting you? Do you expect any of them to initiate coverage?
- Is there anyone else locally who knows your company especially well and might be willing to speak to potential investors?

No hurry with any of this. Thanks in advance for the consideration.

John Rubino
Tel: 804-730-7776

Note that the questions for the investor relations person and the reporter are specific and short, while those directed to the broker are of the more general variety. That's because your broker gets paid for this sort of thing, while the others don't have to answer you and are therefore much more likely to respond to questions with answers that can be looked up in a few minutes.

Concerning the specific Web sites mentioned in this chapter, the same caveat applies as for specific companies: The speed with which things are changing guarantees that some of these sites will be gone before this book hits the stores, with most of the rest either disappearing or morphing into something else a few years later. But the trend toward local information being more and more accessible on-line should continue at least until virtual reality or something even less comprehensible changes the rules once again.

10

BUILDING A
BETTER DATABASE

Investing in local companies involves one risk that has nothing to do with stock prices: information overload.

Plug into your city's financial community without adequate preparation, and the resulting avalanche of annual reports, press releases, analyst reports, E-mail messages and faxes can leave you feeling a little like the sorcerer's apprentice, as if you've conjured up forces beyond your control. More to the point, if you can't keep track of what's coming in, you can't figure out what any of it means. So the time to create a system for managing and analyzing information is before it starts coming. With that in mind, let's begin at the beginning.

Simple Physical Files

If you're not in the habit of filing bills, receipts and insurance forms, you're probably already drowning in paper. So before you start prospecting for local investments, go get a nice big filing cabinet, preferably one that holds legal-sized folders.

Then make a file for each company that looks interesting,

along with each person or organization—your local broker, the chamber, the local venture capital club, your investment club— that might be a useful source. And create a "possibilities" file, where you can dump the names of people, organizations and companies that might be worth checking out in the future. Don't worry if the cabinet starts out mostly empty. You'll fill it.

One last piece of filing cabinet wisdom: Because some pieces of information—prospectuses, annual reports, 10-Ks—are bulky, you'll want to clean out the files periodically. Set a limit of, say, two years for most documents. When they reach retirement age, clear them out to make room for more current information. And when you lose interest in a company, empty its file.

Tools of the Trade

Once the incoming information is organized, you'll need tools for analyzing it. These vary in cost and complexity, from the simplest—paper, pencil and graph paper—all the way out to sophisticated computer software and on-line "applets."

Analyzing stocks the old-fashioned way. Hard as it is to imagine, security analysis was a thriving profession before computers came along. In fact, even before calculators replaced the slide rule. Pre-1980s analysts sketched out charts on graph paper and built income statements and earnings projections on physical spreadsheets. And they benefitted, in the main, from being forced to keep things simple and focus on what was truly important. So if you're a nostalgia buff, or simply not yet computer literate, it's quite possible to follow a group of local companies using such time-tested methods.

A good source of preprinted forms for manual stock analysis is the National Association of Investors Corporation. Its four-page *Stock Selection Guide* walks you through a series of multiple-choice questions that force you to, in effect, compose a company's story. For example:

> The company is (well established) (new) and operates (internationally) (nationally) (regionally). The product line or services is (diversified) (narrow) and sold to (consumers) (manufacturers) (government). . . . The company is (largest) (in top four) (a smaller factor) in its industry.

Along with the questionnaire comes a chart with predrawn growth paths representing rates ranging from 5 percent to 30 percent. Plotting a company's sales and earnings among these lines gives an instant visual representation of its trends. Follow the *Stock Selection Guide*'s instructions, and you'll have created a quite passable analysis of a company's current situation, and used it to make a reasonably well-informed judgment about its likely value in the future.

Computerized spreadsheets. If you have a computer, you can cut the time involved in the above activity with a spreadsheet program like Lotus 1-2-3 or Microsoft Excel. These are basically grids of horizontal and vertical lines that intersect to form cells, which in turn can hold either information that is input by the user or the results of a calculation performed on the contents of other cells. Nearly every new computer comes preloaded with a spreadsheet program, either in stand-alone form or as part of a "suite" of programs, like Microsoft Office or Lotus Smart-Suite.

They vary in bells and whistles, but all do basically the same thing: They take your numbers and manipulate them, and create graphs of the results.

Building a stock analysis spreadsheet from scratch can be laborious. But, luckily, it's also unnecessary. The American Association of Individual Investors (AAII) offers prepackaged template spreadsheets that can be downloaded from its Web site to turn your spreadsheet program into a stock analysis tool instantly. AAII is constantly improving these templates, and as this is written is customizing them for various industries.

Database programs. These are designed to organize names and addresses, which makes them useful for managing your list of sources and companies. They can also swap data with compatible spreadsheets and word processors. So instead of collecting names written on scraps of paper and torn-out articles, save yourself a lot of aggravation by entering them into a simple database, along with their phone numbers and affiliations and a line or two of explanation.

Like spreadsheets, simple database programs come preloaded on most new computers. Virtually all of them are up to the task of tracking a few dozen names and numbers, so going out and actually buying this kind of software is probably something you can avoid.

Financial management software. Next up in power and complexity comes financial management software. Think of these programs, says one reviewer, "as the Swiss Army knife of the investment software arena." They take the basic capabilities of spreadsheets and databases and customize them in ways that make handling all of your finances easier. Among other things, they'll help you set up budgets, balance your checkbook and send checks electronically, paying for themselves in stamp savings alone. They also have modules for retirement planning, mortgage and loan analysis, tax planning and net-worth tracking. In short, they're a lot of fun.

And while these programs aren't written specifically with investors in mind, the latest versions have most of what you'll need, including spreadsheets and charting capabilities, along with the ability to access on-line services and brokers.

Last but not least, because they're geared toward the mass market, they can be bought at computer stores or through catalogs instead of only through the manufacturer. This makes them relatively cheap, and also means that there are books (some of them written by people who can actually write) to assist you in their use.

Portfolio management software. Moving from the general personal-finance program to stand-alone portfolio management software is like going from your family doctor to a specialist. These programs exist only to help investors manage their investments, and this single-task focus lets them cover the subject in much greater detail. For example, they'll handle a wider variety of securities and types of transactions, track more than one portfolio, update portfolios through an on-line service and alert you if a security's price hits some predetermined price level. They'll calculate the rates of return for both individual securities and whole portfolios; produce a calendar listing maturity dates of bonds, options and futures along with expected dividend amounts and payment dates; provide a breakdown of the industries and asset classes of your securities; and include a (I'm simply repeating this without understanding it) flexible cost basis determination procedure.

Of course, power and flexibility are other ways of saying complexity, so mastering portfolio management software takes time and effort. And since most of these programs are sold directly through their producers, you're limited in both where and how you can buy them, and in the amount of reference material that's available. There are two exceptions, however. The NAIC's Investor's Toolkit handles most portfolio management tasks, but because its centerpiece is an automated version of NAIC's simple, useful stock analysis worksheets, it's fairly easy to use. I've tried the demo version, and can attest to the fact that a person of normal intelligence can figure it out in just a few minutes. The AAII, meanwhile, has produced a Fundamental Stock Analysis Disk that automates the security analysis process. Reflecting the different focuses of these two organizations, the NAIC software is probably a better choice for beginners, while AAII's is aimed at computer-literate users.

What's the best way to go? That depends on you. The more computer literate you are, the more comfortable you'll be with sophisticated portfolio management software. The more complex your overall financial life, the more you might benefit from a financial management program like Quicken. But if your purpose is strictly to find and analyze local stocks, the programs offered by NAIC and AAII should be just about all you need.

A few general tips:

- Talk to other investors. Most cities have groups that focus on investment software. They meet regularly to talk about new products and show off innovative ways for using existing software and gadgets. A list of these groups appears on the back cover of each issue of AAII's *Computerized Investing* newsletter. Most of these groups also run computer bulletin boards (BBS), which allow you to pose questions to the groups' resident techies. These BBSs are great sources of software ideas, obviously, but some are also good sources of ideas on local stocks. As you may recall from the previous chapter, the AAII itself runs a BBS that can be reached by computer at (312) 280-8565.

- Try before you buy. Most manufacturers offer demonstration disks of their programs, so ask for one and play with it a while before you make your final purchase. If no demo is available, ask for copies of the reports produced by the program and see if they're what you want. Also note the software manufacturer's return policy—some companies have time limits or charge restocking fees for returned programs.

Investment Software: A Sampling

Personal Finance

Andrew Tobias's Managing Your Money
MECA Software, Inc.
(203) 255-1441
Price: $79.95

Financial Navigator
Financial Navigator International
(800) 468-3636
Price: $495

MacMoney
Survivor Software Limited
(310) 410-9527
Price: $89.95

Quicken Financial Planner
Intuit, Inc.
(800) 624-8742
Price: $59.95

WealthBuilder by *Money* magazine
Reality Technologies, Inc.
(800) 346-2024
Price: $69.95

Stand-Alone Portfolio Management
CAPTOOL
Techserve, Inc.
(800) 826-8082
Price: $129

Fidelity On-line Xpress
Fidelity Investments
(800) 544-0246
Price: $49.95

Market Manager Plus
Dow Jones & Co., Inc.
(800) 815-5100
Price: $299

StreetSmart
Charles Schwab & Co., Inc.
(800) 334-4455
Price: $59

Telescan Portfolio Manager (TPM)
Telescan, Inc.
(800) 324-8246
Price: $395

Wall Street Investor
Comstock Products
(201) 660-9336
Price: $119

Fundamental Valuation

AAII Fundamental Stock Analysis Disk
American Association of Individual Investors
(312) 280-0170
Price: $20

NAIC Investor's Toolkit
National Association of Investors Corp.
(810) 543-0612
Price: $149

STB Prospector
STB Investor Software
A version of NAIC's Investor's Toolkit
(305) 829-2892
Price: $89.00

11

ODDS AND ENDS

One of the problems with writing a narrowly focused investment book is that you glide by many topics that are interesting and useful but which don't quite fit into the main chapters. They deserve—in some cases require—space of their own. But to do them justice where they're first mentioned would involve a Major Digression, a bad idea in this era of shrinking attention spans. So I've lumped these would-be digressions into one chapter, where they can do no harm and, hopefully, a little good. Read on; this is useful stuff, I promise.

Where to Put Your Non–Main Street Capital

Although local stocks represent one of your few legitimate chances of beating the market, *you shouldn't put all your money into them.* Or even most of your money. Your job probably depends on the local economy, and the value of your home certainly does. So a big part of your nest egg should be in things that are influenced by other factors.

But neither should you hand this money over to professional

stock pickers. Because Wall Street's equation of professional-money-management-equals-higher-returns is demonstrably false, your non–Main Street investments should be designed to avoid the fees charged by the pros, while still allowing you to benefit from high-growth (or highly diverse or secure) segments of the global economy. The two best ways to do this are index mutual funds and dividend reinvestment plans.

Index mutual funds. These are mutual funds that don't even try to beat the market. Instead, they simply try to match it by buying a piece of, say, each stock in the S&P 500. Because this requires considerably fewer brain cells than does active stock picking, index funds have relatively low payroll costs. They also do a lot less buying and selling (known as turnover), so they generate lower trading costs and fewer taxable capital gains. Add it all up, and you get a sizable difference in operating costs, a big part of which finds its way into investors' pockets. This advantage ranges, depending on the fund and the method of calculation, from .45 percent of assets each year to nearly 2 percent. Not a big deal in the short run, but over the many years between now and your retirement it can be worth tens of thousands of dollars.

Investors were slow to embrace indexing, but lately they've come around. By mid–1997 the Vanguard Index 500 was the second biggest mutual fund of any kind, with nearly $35 billion in assets. And Vanguard, the king of indexing, was threatening to surpass Fidelity as the overall leader in the mutual fund business.

Since there are now index funds of every flavor, it's possible to build a portfolio that provides growth and diversification while costing only a fraction of what a similar group of actively managed funds would charge. Comprehensive stats on index funds are compiled in *Morningstar's Mutual Funds*, available in most public libraries. They're also available on just about any good financial Web site. Here's a list of established, highly rated index funds:

Table 11.1
TEN SOLID INDEX FUNDS

Company	Av. annual % return over 3 years ending 3/31/97	Assets ($ mil.)	Expense ratio	Phone number
Vanguard Index Growth	23.95	1,067.4	0.20	800-662-7447
Vanguard Index 500	22.18	34,587.2	0.20	800-662-7447
Pegasus Equity Index I	22.15	636.6	0.15	800-688-3550
BT Investment Equity 500 Index	22.00	494.7	0.25	800-730-1313
Benchmark Equity Index A	22.00	712.3	0.22	800-621-2550
California Investment S&P 500	21.97	58.4	0.22	800-225-8778
First American Equity Index C	21.89	417.0	0.35	800-637-2548
Nations Equity—Index Prime A	21.88	601.2	0.35	800-321-7854
MasterWorks S&P 500 Stock	21.78	1,422.2	0.20	800-776-0179
Prudential Stock Index Z	21.65	262.1	0.60	800-225-1852

Source: *Morningstar*

Next, consider foreign index funds. Americans, understandably, tend to forget just how much is happening beyond our borders. That's a mistake. The United States stock market, huge though it is, accounts for only 40 percent of the world's market capitalization. According to a recent survey by *Fortune* magazine, thirty-nine of the world's fifty largest companies are based overseas. And despite a raging bull market here at home, the United States isn't even in the top five for total return so far in the 1990s. Instead, the big winners are "developing" countries, such as Brazil, China and Chile, which are starting from such a low economic base that their growth, in percentage terms, far exceeds ours. Their stock markets are so small—remember, the value of the entire Indian market is less than that of General Electric—that they absolutely explode when the global smart money notices them.

To grasp the potential of today's developing markets, consider those of yesteryear: A $10,000 bet on Japan's market in 1970 would have grown to $130,000 by 1990; $10,000 invested in Hong Kong in 1980 ballooned to $50,000 by that decade's end. Both growth rates put the United States to shame over the same periods.

With much of the world now emulating these two success stories, there's serious money to be made out there. But as Ronald Reagan used to say about balancing the budget, how you do it makes all the difference. International investing involves several risks that aren't present domestically. Currency fluctuations, for instance, frequently wipe out otherwise good gains. And even highly advanced nations can screw up royally. Japan, to take the most notable example, fell from the stratosphere to the basement during the 1990s.

As for those developing countries, think of them as adolescents with nuclear weapons instead of car keys and you get the general picture: China is a dictatorship in which the government can arbitrarily change the rules of business; India is so mired in bureaucracy that few know with certainty what the rules are; and

Russia is pioneering the intriguing concept of "gangster capital-ism," in which car bombs and automatic weapons have replaced proxy votes in corporate etiquette. Each country, amazingly, has done well by its investors during at least part of the past decade, but none is guaranteed to survive in its current form.

So treat emerging countries like emerging companies. Begin with diversified global or regional index funds, and when you start looking at individual country funds, buy a lot of them, in different regions, to minimize country-specific risk.

Dividend Reinvestment Plans (DRIPs). After buying as little as one share of many companies' stock, it's possible to have the company convert future dividends into more shares, commis-sion-free. This allows you to set up a portfolio that grows au-tomatically, bypassing even the minimal fees charged by index funds. DRIPs have drawbacks, however. To participate, the stock must generally be registered in your name, rather than its "street name," as when it's held by a broker. This means you have to take physical possession of the stock certificate. So building a diversified DRIP portfolio in the traditional manner involves an inordinate amount of paperwork.

To get around this, the NAIC offers a Low Cost Investing Plan, which, for a very modest fee, enables its members to buy into a wide variety of DRIPs without the clerical hassles in-volved in going it alone. Participants can buy as little as one share of a given company's stock to begin. And NAIC handles the paperwork. Besides the NAIC, the best sources of infor-mation on DRIPs are *The Moneypaper* and *DRIP Investor*, a pair of newsletters that track this market and offer advice on how best to play it.

NO-LOAD STOCKS. A growing number of companies have taken their DRIP programs to their logical conclusion by selling stock directly to the public, free of any brokerage commissions. Hence the term no-load stock.

Buying one of these is like buying a mutual fund: Call a toll-free number and ask for plan information, fill out a form and mail a check. According to Charles Carlson, publisher of *DRIP Investor* and several books on this subject, recent regulatory changes are causing the number of no-load stocks to explode. By 1997 there were 320, up from 52 in 1994. And "I expect to see 750 to 1,000 in two years," he says.

In the meantime, here's a portfolio of his favorite no-loads:

Table 11.2
TEN GOOD NO-LOAD STOCKS

Company	*Initial minimum investment ($)*	*Subsequent minimum investment ($)*	*Telephone number*
Exxon	250	50	800-252-1800
Regions Financial	500	25	800-922-3468
Reuters Holdings	250	50	800-774-4117
Procter & Gamble	250	100	800-764-7483
Lucent Technologies	1,000	100	800-582-3686
Merk & Co.	350	50	800-774-4117
Southern Co.	250	25	800-774-4117
BellSouth	500	50	888-887-2965
McDonald's	1,000	100	800-774-4117
Home Depot	250	25	800-774-4117

Source: *DRIP Investor*

This portfolio can be created for $4,600 up front. Because it's made up of stocks from a wide variety of industries, it's well diversified. And because the dividends are automatically reinvested in more stock, it will grow without another minute of your time, and virtually without charging you a penny in fees.

Asset Allocation

Establishing a mix of index funds and no-load stocks that suits your situation and temperament is called asset allocation. Doing it right requires a grasp of three interrelated concepts:

Compounding. When something grows at a constant rate (i.e. exponentially), it doubles in a fixed number of years. For example, earning a steady 10.5 percent annually—or about what common stocks in general have returned in this century—doubles your money in just under 7 years. Then the real fun begins, because each successive doubling is on a larger base: In 21 years, you've got eight times your original stake; in forty years, $1,000 grows to $54,000.

Chart 11.1

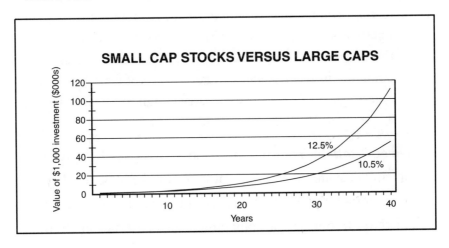

Now notice what happens when you replace 10.5 percent with the 12.5 percent that faster-growing small-cap stocks have generated. Your money doubles in 5.8 years rather than 7 years. A small difference in the short run, but after 40 years it produces an extra doubling. Instead of $54,000, that initial $1,000 becomes $111,000. The conclusion: Small differences in a portfolio's rate of growth will, given enough time, produce huge differences in the final result.

Risk. Investors face three kinds of risk:

- *Market risk* refers to the ups and downs of a given asset class, like stocks or bonds. The higher returns that stocks have generated, for instance, come with a corresponding increase in volatility, which is another way of saying that stocks in the aggregate bounce around a lot more than bonds or money market funds. The Dow Jones Industrial Average, for instance, has fallen by 10 percent or more fifty times in this century, and by 25 percent fifteen times.
- *Company-specific risk* covers all the bad things that can happen to a given stock. Over the years, many, many stocks have gone to zero, wiping out everything their investors put in.
- *Inflation* is the erosion of purchasing power that comes from the dollar's long-term decline in value. Think of it as compounding in reverse, and you get an idea of what happens to a nest egg that's not growing fast enough to offset inflation.

Diversification. You minimize the above risks by spreading your capital around in various ways. For market risk, divide your savings among stocks, bonds, cash and real estate. This way, good times in one sector compensate for bad times in another.

To minimize company-specific risk, own a lot of different stocks, divided among industries that are not subject to the same macroeconomic influences. And to offset inflation, hold a sufficient amount of fast-growing assets, like small-cap stocks.

To translate the above into an asset allocation plan, you've got to begin with an understanding of which kind of risk applies to you.

If you expect to draw on your savings within a few years, your enemy is the cyclical downturn that, roughly twice a decade, slices a fifth or so off the value of most common stocks. For the short-term investor, this loss is effectively permanent. So it's logical and prudent to diversify into things that aren't affected by bear markets, like cash, bonds and conservative stocks with high dividend yields.

If you have a longer time horizon, say, a decade or more, market fluctuations are irrelevant. Instead, your main problem is the erosion of purchasing power caused by inflation. And the way to eliminate this risk is by concentrating on things that are growing fast enough to more than offset inflation. At this point in human history, that means growth stocks. A reasonable thirty-five-year-old's portfolio should therefore look very different from that of an equally reasonable sixty-year-old. For example, see Chart 11.2.

Chart 11.2

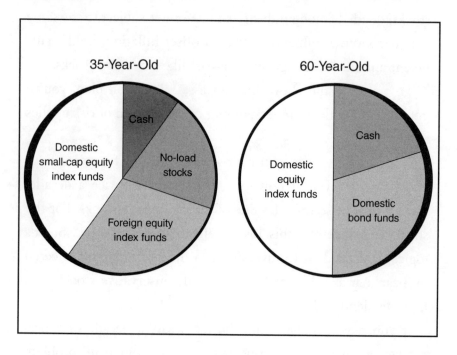

Diversification within your stock portfolio. For the part of
your portfolio that's in individual stocks, whether no-loads or
local emerging growth, you'll want to minimize the risk of any
one of them blowing up by having at least five, and preferably
ten, different positions. I can't stress the point strongly enough
that any company, no matter how good it looks, can fail, taking
its investors on a permanent one-way ride to oblivion. For an
example of this, recall Omni Multimedia, which was discussed
in chapter 7's look at management quality.

Back in 1995, Omni seemed a fairly safe bet, as emerging
companies go. It was expanding in a growing field where it
was already successful, it was covered by a local analyst who was
bullish, it was getting good local press and management was

making projections that, if realized, would surely send the stock higher. Then everything that could go wrong did, and the stock—well, you can see what happened in chart 11.3. So next time you discover a sure thing and are tempted to put more than 10 percent of your capital into it, pull out this chart and stare at it until the urge goes away.

Chart 11.3 OMNI MULTIMEDIA

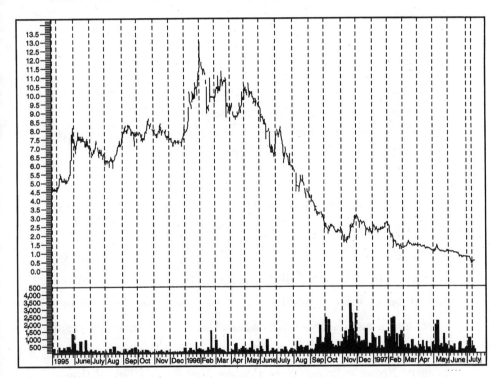

Insider Trading

Now let's revisit your stressed-out brother-in-law. Recall from chapter 4 that he slumps into your easy chair and groans, "This job is killing me." Good local investor that you are, you gently tease the story out of him. "GE Capital just offered to buy us out for thirty dollars a share," he finally says. "My boss is running around like crazy trying to figure out if that's a fair price, and I'm left doing all his work."

You surreptitiously reach for the local paper and see that the current price is twenty dollars. You then excuse yourself to go to the bathroom, but detour into the bedroom, where you call your broker and buy as much stock as possible in your brother-in-law's company.

Have you:

A. Made a brilliant move that both makes you some serious money and validates the premise of this book?

B. Committed a crime that could earn both you and your brother-in-law a vacation at Club Fed?

If you're not sure, don't worry. Even the experts disagree on what constitutes illegal insider trading. Sill, when you're looking for information that hasn't yet been widely disseminated, as you certainly are if you're following the advice given here, you've got to be at least generally aware of where the line between smart and illegal is drawn this week. Here's a definition of inside information, courtesy of the *Association of Investment and Management Research Standards of Practice Handbook*, 1996 edition:

"Inside information" is generally defined as information about a company that is both material and nonpublic. Under the securities laws of the United States, information is material if a reasonable investor is likely to consider it significant in making an investment decision or if the information is reasonably certain to have a substantial impact on the market price of a company's securities. Information is nonpublic if it has not been generally disclosed to the marketplace. To become public, information must be disseminated so that it is reasonably available to investors generally. The disclosure of information by a corporate insider to a select group of analysts is not sufficient to make that information public under U.S. securities laws.

Since your brother-in-law is an insider, and since the information is definitely both material and nonpublic, you would, as it turns out, indeed be committing a crime by buying the stock. With this in mind, let's sketch out some rules governing the differences between legal and illegal trading:

- Information that comes to you via a confidential relationship, such as lawyer/client or doctor/patient, cannot be used.
- Neither can the following, until they're made public: a big new order; changes in dividend policy; an acquisition; the loss of a major contract; a default on debt; a major corporate reorganization; knowledge of forthcoming press coverage, whether it's favorable or not; big changes in corporate earnings projections; regulatory approvals of new products. There are more, but you get the idea. If something is a discreet event, and it matters in a big way, and it hasn't been announced publicly, then it's inside information, and acting on it is legally dicey.

On the other hand, things that have to do with trends rather than events are relatively safe. For instance, if a customer is stepping up its orders from your firm, that's a perfectly legal signal, because "improving business" probably doesn't constitute nonpublic news.

Financial Shenanigans

In the mountains of information that the SEC requires companies to make public, some of the most useful stuff appears in the most obscure places, like annual report footnotes and proxies. And so most of it is ignored, just as the companies hope it will be. But if you're the sort who likes to unravel mysteries and dig deeper than most, there are treasures buried in those documents.

One example comes from Jeffrey Saut, former research director of Ferris Baker Watts, a Washington, D.C.–based investment bank. A few years back, Saut was looking for some emerging agriculture companies. And he found one that, on the surface, had the goods: Crop Growers, an insurance company based in Montana, was growing dramatically by insuring farmers' crops against drought and flood. The crop-insurance business was highly profitable, and Crop Growers was taking market share from slower rivals. It looked in many ways like a classic emerging growth story, and, at thirty dollars a share, appeared to be reasonably valued on prospective earnings.

But before jumping in, Saut did something that most investors rarely do: He read the company's proxy. This is a document that invites shareholders to the annual meeting and tells the world how much money the guys running the company make, among other things. And there Saut found some things that stopped him cold: Crop Growers had made interest-free loans to its officers, had cut deals with companies owned by these same officers and in any event paid its top people "high salaries in relation to the size and performance of the company," he recalls. The proxy also disclosed a big-bucks relationship with Tony Coelho, a lobbyist who had previously resigned from Congress under a financial cloud.

Individually, each of these things might have been overlooked, says Saut, but "in the aggregate, it smelled." He passed on Crop Growers, and watched from the sidelines as it had a string of problems, beginning with some overly optimistic earnings projections, and ending, for all intents and purposes, with the indictment of its top people for improper campaign contributions. The company's market value plunged by two-thirds, where it languished until it was taken over by a competitor for about eleven dollars a share.

Not surprisingly, Saut urges serious investors to give the proxy a once-over before committing to an emerging company. Even the process of getting a proxy can be telling. "A lot of companies won't send you their proxies when you ask for an analyst's package. A lot will tell you 'We only send those to stockholders,' or 'We're out of them.' " This, he says, "is a red flag."

Now, there are so many ways for companies to hide incriminating facts that it's impossible to list them all here (even if I could, accountants would find a few dozen new ones by the time this is published). But one fellow who comes close to covering all the bases is Howard Schilit. His book *Financial Shenanigans* is a big help if you really want to know what your investments are up to. Here's how he introduces his approach:

> If the Food and Drug Administration rather than the Securities and Exchange Commission (SEC) regulated financial reporting, you might see this warning on each financial report: BEWARE: RELYING ON THIS REPORT COULD BE HAZARDOUS TO YOUR WEALTH.
>
> This label would alert investors and lenders to the substantial risks of relying on financial reports, whether audited or not. For example, they may fail to alert investors and lenders to a company's financial difficulties, they may fail to measure a company's actual financial performance and its economic condition accurately; or they may simply be incomplete.

Schilit considers the top five shenanigans to be:

Recording revenue too soon
Recording bogus revenues
Boosting income with one-time gains
Shifting current expenses to a later period
Failing to record or disclose all liabilities

Recording revenue too soon, for instance, is often accomplished by shipping goods before a sale is finalized or by counting a sale as final when important uncertainties exist or when future services are still due. In English, when a company sells something, it receives cash. But it doesn't necessarily get to keep it all. In many businesses, such as, say, software and publishing, a significant part of each shipment is returned for refunds. Or the sale might bring with it an obligation on the part of the company that eventually costs it money, as with car warranties. In the first instance, real revenues are actually less than cash initially received. In the second, liabilities are actually higher than would be apparent if the company recorded only the sales number. Either way, the results look better in the short run than they eventually turn out to be.

For an example of Shenanigan number four—shifting current expenses to a later period—consider America Online. The pioneering on-line service had reported growing profits during its rise, but it did so by writing off the cost of luring new subscribers over two years. Had it taken its marketing costs as they occurred, it would have reported consistent losses rather than rising profits. And when, under pressure from the financial community, it finally switched to a more conservative accounting stance, the result was a huge write-off that wiped out the past several years' reported earnings.

IPOs

Initial public offerings, or IPOs, are something you'll see a lot of once you start looking around locally. These are formerly private companies that have done well enough in the past few years to enable them to sell stock to the public.

And since an offering prospectus is similar in format and content to a 10-K report, you can analyze IPOs just as you would any other emerging growth stock, with one big addition: You've also got to investigate the underwriter. This is the investment bank that manages a company's IPO, placing its stock in the hands of investors and promising to "make a market" in the shares. That means it stands ready to buy and sell the stock, usually maintaining an inventory of shares on hand. So, if an investor wants to sell, he is assured of a price—not necessarily a good one, but one that bears at least some relationship to recent history. If, on the other hand, the underwriter shirks its responsibilities, a new stock can languish because it lacks a source of institutional research and a coherent market for its shares.

A graphic example of this is n-Vision. Formerly a division of military contractor Advanced Technologies, it made virtual reality gear that had some obvious nonmilitary uses. To tap the commercial market, ATS spun off n-Vision in 1996 and took it public for five dollars a share. The initial demand for its equipment was good, and since nothing is sexier than virtual reality, the stock doubled in early trading. But then n-Vision's underwriter, Manhattan-based Stratton, Oakmont, ran afoul of the Securities and Exchange Commission and was shut down. Its inventory of n-Vision stock was handed off to J. B. Oxford, another broker, which, according to n-Vision management, then dumped it, sending the price into freefall.

In mid-1997, n-Vision was a healthy company by some measures. Its sales had risen by 142 percent in the year's first quarter and its start-up losses were falling, pretty much in line with what was expected when the stock was ten dollars. And yet the stock could be had for 50 cents, when it traded at all, which was infrequently indeed. "With nobody representing you on Wall Street, your stock's not worth very much," says n-Vision's chagrined president.

So before buying an IPO, check out the underwriter, including how long they've been at it, how many other deals they've done and how those stocks have traded. If they've abandoned their previous clients, then wait a while, and you may be able to buy the stock a whole lot cheaper. If, on the other hand, the investment bank has a track record of bringing to market companies that subsequently did very well, then the riskiness of the stock in question just went down.

Convertible Bonds: The Best of Both Worlds?

"Converts" have a seductive premise. They're bonds, so you get interest payments and a legal status that's senior to equity in the event of bankruptcy. And they're convertible into stock, so they have the upside potential of equity. Lots of emerging companies have issued such securities, so you'll want to be able to value them in relation to the underlying stock.

For example, let's take a $1,000 bond with a 7 percent coupon that's convertible into 50 shares of stock. The stock currently sells for $15, so the convertible's underlying stock is worth $750 (50 × 15). When you buy the bond you pay $250 more than you would for 50 shares of stock. But you get $70 a year in extra income. Now divide $250 by $70 for the number of years (3.5) it will take for the interest to pay off the premium. Looked at another way, in buying the bond you're paying a 33 percent premium over the current price of the stock ($1,000/$750).

To summarize, you've got two indicators: the number of years it takes the bond coupon to pay off the premium, and the percentage premium over the share price. The closer these get to zero, the more attractive is the convertible.

For a quick way to do these calculations, along with a lot of good background information, check out Numa Financial Systems' Web site: http://www.numa.com/derivs/ref/calculat/cb/calc-cba.htm.

Leverage: The Crack Cocaine of the Investment World

After your first big winner, you're going to feel the most delicious sensation in finance: a sense of omniscience. "You did it once," a tiny voice will whisper, "and you can do it again." And again. So why not speed up the process with a little "margin," or some of those "derivatives" you hear so much about?

This voice is evil. When you hear it, take your motorcycle for a rush-hour spin on the freeway, send your boss's spouse a suggestive E-mail, do anything but call your broker. Leverage is the crack cocaine of the investment world, and it will warp your perspective just as completely as will the real thing. Here's a crash—pun intended—course in what to avoid:

Margin. This refers to the act of borrowing against securities in a brokerage account. Yes, your broker will loan you 50 percent of the value of the stocks you own, no questions asked. Mature investors with stable portfolios often find this a cheap alternative to, say, a car loan. But because margin magnifies the volatility of your portfolio, even a normal correction can earn you a "margin call," wherein your broker will give you a choice of either sending more money to cover your debts or selling some stock in a down market. Selling at the bottom is exactly what you want to avoid.

Derivatives. Dangerous though margin is, it's kid stuff compared to derivatives. These include options, futures contracts, warrants and their even more exotic cousins, all of which derive their value from underlying stocks or commodities (hence the name *derivative*). And they all move much more violently than whatever they're linked to. In the case of options, you can lose your entire investment in a matter of months. With futures contracts, you can lose more than your original investment. Like margin, derivatives can turn a normal trading decline into a permanent loss. As such, they're not worth the risk. Ever.

Now, having said that, I realize that the voice of Satan will win with some readers. So, if you have to spice up your life with leverage, at least educate yourself. The following Web site, created by Numa Financial Systems, is a good starting point: http://www.numa.com/overview/overview.htm.

12

LOCAL INVESTING IN A NUTSHELL

This book has thrown a lot of information at you, enough to make buying local stocks seem more than a little forbidding. But strip away the statistics and anecdotes and you'll find that only a few fairly simple steps are really necessary. Here they are:

Category One: Plug into the local investment community
- Choose a local business journal.
- Open an account with a local broker.
- Compile a list of local stocks from the business journal's list of fastest growing companies and your broker's recommended list.
- Call the companies and ask for information packets.
- Read the company literature and narrow the list to the best prospects. Call them and ask to be placed on their mailing lists.
- Do basic security analysis on these companies.

- Instruct your broker to buy the stocks that look the most interesting.

Category Two: Acquire the right tools

- Buy a filing cabinet that holds legal-sized paper.
- Choose security analysis tools, such as manual graphs and charts, spreadsheet software or portfolio management software.
- Learn to navigate cyberspace: Get a computer with a fast modem, sign up for an Internet account and master the basics of search engines, bookmarking and E-mail.
- Find the Web sites of your business journal, brokerage house and the companies you're following, and save them for future reference.
- Choose a good financial Web site and set up a portfolio that includes your favorite local companies. Have the site generate price updates on demand and notify you of relevant news.

Category Three: Some advanced strategies

- Analyze the local economy: Do one or two industries dominate? Which technologies/markets must you understand to make informed judgments? Which companies are the main local players and who knows them best?
- Join or form an investment club that focuses on local companies.
- Join a venture capital club.
- Join the chamber of commerce.

And, finally, remember that investing on Main Street is a never-ending game. Every day, for the rest of your life, new companies will be born nearby, new people will discover them and new sources of information will come into being. But the same basic rule will apply: The better connected you are to the local economy, the more companies you'll catch on the way up. Eventually, the next Wal-Mart will emerge nearby, and you'll be there. Guaranteed.

ACKNOWLEDGMENTS

This book would not have happened without the advice and support of three people: James Bacon, publisher of *Virginia Business Magazine*, who sent me into the heart of the local investment community; Paul Aron, who dug into his worth-its-weight-in-gold Rolodex for the names of several talented agents; and Faith Hamlin, the agent at the top of Paul's list, who saw some value here and opened numerous doors to make it a reality.

Thanks to the folks at Equis International for letting me use their superb MetaStock software to create the price charts in this book. And special thanks to my editors, Henry Ferris and Ann Treistman, for vastly improving what I sent them.

APPENDIX A:
LOCAL SOURCES

The following is a list of local sources of investment information from selected area codes around the country. Where the name of an organization isn't a clear indication of its purpose, I've added one of two notations:

RB: Regional or local brokerage house
VCC: Venture capital club, network or similar organization

For entities that don't fit into these categories, I've included an explanation with the entry.

The business journals were derived from lists provided by the Network of City Business Journals and the Association of Area Business Publications, along with the results of a national Yellow Pages search under "Business Journal" and a lot of calling around.

The brokers were obtained from local business journal Books of Lists, and by calls to business journal editors and the brokerage houses themselves.

Venture capital clubs came from lists compiled by the University of New Hampshire's Center for Venture Studies and International Capital Resources, a California venture firm. Venture capital clubs are often run by people with other jobs, so where possible I've included the name of the club manager. When you call such a club, don't be surprised if the receptionist announces that you've reached a local law or investment firm. And be prepared to ask for the person, not the club.

You'll notice that occasionally a resource is given that isn't located in the area specified. I've done this where local information is available from an outside source.

Alabama
Area Code 205 (Birmingham)
Birmingham Business Journal (205-322-0000; http://www.bbj.com)
Business Alabama magazine (205-941-1425)

Morgan Keegan RB (800-366-7426; http://www.morgankeegan.com)
Robinson Humphrey RB (205-533-2150)
Sterne Agee & Leach RB (205-252-5900)

Birmingham Venture Club
c/o Birmingham Chamber (205-323-5461)

Birmingham Area Chamber (205-323-5461)

Area Code 334 (Mobile, Montgomery)
Morgan Keegan RB (800-366-7426; http://www.morgankeegan.com)
Sterne Agee & Leach RB (334-263-3892)

Montgomery Chamber (334-834-5200)

Alaska
Alaska Business Monthly—Woodinville, WA (206-483-9705)

Area Code 907
Journal of Commerce—Anchorage (907-561-4772)

Wedbush Morgan Securities RB (907-452-8101)

Alaska Investnet VCC (907-463-3929; http://www.ptialaska.net/~jedc)

Alaska State Chamber (907-278-2722)
Anchorage Chamber (907-272-2401)

Arizona
Area Code 602 (Phoenix, Mesa, Scottsdale, Tempe)
Arizona Business Gazette (602-271-7301; http://www.azcentral.com)
Business Journal (602-230-8400)

McKee (W.B.) Securities RB (602-954-7365)
Peacock, Hislop, Staley & Given RB (602-952-6800)
Piper Jaffray RB (602-815-8700)
Round Hill Securities RB (800-869-8834)
Wedbush Morgan Securities RB (602-956-9470)

Investment Exchange VCC (800-563-5448)

Arizona Chamber (602-248-9172)
Mesa Chamber (602-969-1307)
Phoenix Chamber (602-254-5521)
Scottsdale Chamber (602-945-8481)
Tempe Chamber (602-967-7891)

Area Code 520 (Tucson)
Inside Tucson Business (520-294-1200; http://www.azbiz.com)

Tucson Metro Chamber (520-792-1212)

Arkansas
Area Code 501
Arkansas Business (501-587-0341; http://www.abnews.com)

Boatmen's Investment Services RB (501-378-1132)
Morgan Keegan RB (800-366-7426; http://www.morgankeegan.com)
Stephens & Co. RB (501-377-2000)

Arkansas State Chamber—Little Rock (501-374-9225)

California
Area Code 209
Business Journal—Fresno (209-237-0114)
Business Tribune—Modesto (209-544-2030)
Business Journal—Stockton (209-476-0861)
Business Journal—Visalia (209-627-9170)

Van Kasper & Co. RB (209-244-6828; http://www.vkco.com)

Fresno Chamber (209-233-4651)
Stockton Chamber (209-547-2770)

Area Code 213 (Los Angeles)
Los Angeles Business Journal (213-549-5225)
San Fernando Business Journal (213-549-5225)

Wedbush Morgan Securities RB (213-688-8000)

Los Angeles Chamber (213-629-0676)
Wilshire Chamber (213-386-8224)

Area Code 310 (Los Angeles, Long Beach)
Long Beach Business Journal (310-988-1222)

Cruttenden, Roth RB (310-235-2188)
Van Kasper & Co. RB (310-820-2970; http://www.vkco.com)

Brentwood Area Chamber (310-476-4573)
Long Beach Area Chamber (310-437-4517)
South Bay Association Chamber—Torrance (310-515-2558)
West L.A. Chamber (310-477-9994)

Area Code 408
Business Journal—San Jose (408-295-3800; http://www.amcity.com.sanjose)

Van Kasper & Co. RB (408-947-3850; http://www.vkco.com)
Wedbush Morgan Securities RB (408-776-3245)

Silicon Valley Capital Club VCC (408-971-9300)

Cupertino Chamber (408-252-7054)
Milpitas Chamber (408-262-2613)
Saratoga Chamber (408-867-0753)
Sunnyvale Chamber (408-736-4971)

Area Code 415 (San Francisco)
Red Chip Review (small-cap newsletter based in Portland) (503-241-1265)
San Francisco Business Times (415-989-2522)

Hambrecht and Quist RB (415-986-5500)
Montgomery Securities RB (415-627-2000; http://www.montgomery.com)
Van Kasper & Co RB (415-391-5600; http://www.vkco.com)
Wedbush Morgan Securities RB (415-986-3330)

California Capital Network VCC (415-296-2519)

Los Altos Chamber (415-948-1455)
Melno Park Chamber (415-363-2818)
Palo Alto Chamber (415-324-3121)
San Francisco Chamber (415-392-4511)

Area Code 510
Van Kasper & Co. RB (510-932-0728; http://www.vkco.com)

Fremont Chamber (510-795-2244)
Livermore Chamber (510-447-1606)
Oakland Chamber (510-874-4800)

Area Code 619 (San Diego)
San Diego Business Journal (619-277-6359)
Southwest Business Reports—San Diego (619-296-7700)

Leedoms San Diego Stock Report (newsletter) (619-622-0321)
San Diego Source (city Web site) (http://www.sddt.com)

Brookstreet Securities RB (619-696-9438)
Hambrecht & Quist RB (619-546-8181)
Torrey Pines Securities RB (619-259-9921)
Wedbush Morgan Securities RB (619-233-9600)

Chula Vista Chamber (619-420-6602)
Greater San Diego Chamber (619-232-0124)
Peninsula Chamber (619-223-9767)
San Diego Chamber (619-232-0124)

Area Code 707
Business Journal—Santa Rosa (707-579-2900)
Sonoma Business Magazine—Santa Rosa (707-575-8282)

Foothill Securities RB (707-542-9449)

Area Code 714
Orange County Business Journal (714-833-8373)

Cruttenden, Roth RB (714-757-5700)
Wedbush Morgan Securities RB (714-759-1311)

Orange County Venture Forum VCC (714-855-0652)
Pacific Venture Capital Network VCC (714-753-0490)

Anaheim Chamber (714-758-0222)
Huntington Beach Chamber (714-536-8888)
Santa Ana Chamber (714-541-5353)

Area Code 805
Businesscents Magazine (805-324-2333)
Hispanic Business (805-682-5843)
Strictly Business magazine (805-922-9791)

Brookstreet Securities RB (805-934-1021)
Cruttenden, Roth RB (805-963-1473)

Bakersfield Chamber (805-327-4421)
North of the River Chamber (805-393-4556)
Oxnard Chamber (805-385-8860)

Area Code 909
Valley Business Journal (909-676-7082)

Pomona Chamber (909-622-1256)
Riverside Chamber (909-683-7100)

Area Code 916
Business Journal of Sacramento (916-447-7661)
North Valley Business Journal (916-342-7160)

California Chamber—Sacramento (916-856-5200)
Sacramento Chamber (916-443-3771)
Sacramento Metro Chamber (916-552-6800)

Colorado
Area Code 303 (Denver)
Boulder County Business Report (303-440-4952)
Colorado Business Magazine (303-397-7600; http://cobizmag.com)
Denver Business Journal (303-837-3500)
Rocky Mountain News (303-892-5000)

Neidiger Tucker Bruner RB (303-623-5074)
Wedbush Morgan Securities RB (303-571-4949)

Rockies Venture Club (303-831-4174)

Aurora Chamber (303-755-5000)
Denver Chamber (303-450-0335)
Denver Metro Chamber (303-534-8500)
Englewood Chamber (303-789-4473)

Area Code 970
Four Corners Business Journal (970-385-7883)
Grand Valley Business Times (970-241-0177)

Connecticut
Area Code 203
Greater New Haven Chamber (203-787-6735)
Stratford Chamber (203-335-3800)

Area Code 860
Hartford Business Journal (860-236-9998)

Advest RB (800-508-1000)
Buell Securities RB (860-258-2300)
Coburn & Meredith RB (860-522-7171)
First Albany RB (860-293-3000)

Greater Hartford Chamber (860-525-4451)

Delaware
Area Code 302
Delaware Business Review (800-282-8586)

Delaware Entrepreneurs' Forum VCC (302-652-4241)

Florida
Area Code 305
Miami Daily Business Review (305-377-3721)

Raymond James RB (305-461-1200)

Florida Venture Council Forum VCC (305-446-5060)

Gold Coast Chamber (305-866-6020)
North Dade Chamber (305-949-3355)

Area Code 407
Brevard Business News (407-951-7777)
Orlando Business Journal (407-649-8470)

Raymond James RB (800-426-7449)

East Orange Chamber (407-277-5951)

Area Code 561
Raymond James RB (561-835-1040)

Boca Raton Chamber (561-395-4433)

Area Code 813
Florida Trend magazine (813-821-5800; http://www.fltrend.com)
Tampa Bay Business Journal (813-873-8225)

Raymond James RB (800-248-8863)

St. Pete Chamber (813-821-4715)
Tampa Chamber (813-228-0606)

Area Code 904
Jacksonville Business Journal (904-396-3502)

Alex Brown & Sons RB (904-355-0643; ask for Gooch Milam)
Allen Ewing, Inc. RB (904-354-5573)

First Coast Venture Capital Group (904-642-4840)

Capital City Chamber (904-224-0152)
Florida Chamber (904-425-1200)
Jacksonville Chamber (904-366-6600)
Tallahassee Area Chamber (904-224-8116)

Area Code 941
Business People Magazine (941-277-1144)
Lee Business Digest (941-481-9441)
Sarasota Business Journal (941-378-9048)
Southwest Florida Business Magazine (941-277-1144)

Raymond James RB (941-649-0900)

Area Code 954
Broward Daily Business Review (954-468-2600)
South Florida Business Journal (954-359-2100)

Raymond James RB (800-334-2777)

Fort Lauderdale Chamber (954-462-6000)
Hallandale Chamber (954-454-0541)
South Florida Chamber (954-423-1750)

Georgia
Area Codes 404, 770 (Atlanta)
Atlanta Business Chronicle (404-249-1000)
Business Ledger (770-719-1819)
Business Post (770-442-3278)
Georgia Trend magazine (770-931-9410)

Raymond James RB (404-365-9712)
Robinson Humphrey RB (404-266-6000)
Stern Agee & Leach RB (404-365-9630)

Atlanta Venture Forum VCC (404-873-8522)

Atlanta Chamber (404-880-9000)

Area Code 706 (Augusta, Columbus)
Business Journal (706-650-3137)

Columbus Chamber (706-327-1566)

Area Code 912 (Savannah)
Coastal Business Chronicle (912-352-4699)
Mount Vernon Business Ledger (912-583-4914)
Savannah Business Journal (912-354-5553)

Robinson Humphrey RB (912-355-6608)

Savannah Area Chamber (912-944-0444)

Hawaii
Area Code 808
Pacific Business News (808-596-2021)

Wedbush Morgan Securities RB (808-536-4579)

Hawaii Chamber (808-533-3181)

Idaho
Area Code 208
North Idaho Business Journal (208-664-8176)
Marple's Business Newsletter (206-281-9609)

Boise Chamber (208-378-8700)

Illinois
Area Code 217
Springfield Business Journal (217-544-7400)

Area Code 312
Crain's Chicago Business (312-649-5370)

Barrington Research RB (312-634-6358)
William Blair & Co. RB (312-236-1600)

Chicagoland Chamber (312-494-6700)
Cosmopolitan Chamber (312-786-0212)
Illinois Chamber (312-983-7100)
Southwest Chicago Chamber (312-476-6090)

Other Area Codes
Dupage Business Ledger (630-571-8911)

Rockford Area Chamber (815-987-8100)

Indiana
Area Code 219
Michiana Investment Network c/o Caroline Anderson VCC (219-282-4350)

Area Code 317
Indiana Business Magazine (317-692-1200)
Indianapolis Business Journal (317-634-6200; http://www.ibj.com)

Hilliard Lyons RB (800-444-1854)
NatCity Investments RB (800-382-1126)
Ohio Company RB (317-632-7712)

Great Midwest Venture Capital Conference (317-264-2820)
Venture Club of Indiana c/o Margo Jaqua VCC (317-253-1244)

Indiana Chamber (317-264-3110)
Indianapolis Chamber (317-464-2200)

Area Code 812
Private Investors Network VCC (812-339-8937)

Bloomington Chamber (812-336-6381)
Evansville Chamber (812-425-8147)

Iowa
Area Code 319
Cedar Rapids Chamber (319-398-5317)

Area Code 515
Des Moines Business Record (515-288-3336)

Venture Network of Iowa c/o Phyllis Beamer VCC (515-286-4933)

Kansas
Area Code 316
Wichita Business Journal (316-267-6406)

Perkins Smart & Boyd RB (316-263-8444)
Primeline Securities RB (316-269-2400)

Wichita Area Chamber (316-265-7771)

Area Code 913
Johnson County Business Times (913-649-8778)

Perkins Smart & Boyd RB (913-384-5900)

Kansas Venture Capital Network c/o Steve Kelly VCC (913-296-5298)

Kansas Chamber (913-357-6321)
Kansas City Chamber (913-371-3070)

Kentucky
Area Code 502
Business First—Louisville (502-583-1731)

Hilliard Lyons RB (502-588-8400)

Kentucky Investment Capital Forum c/o Norris Christian VCC (800-626-2930)
c/o Rebecca Craig Venture Club VCC (502-589-6868)

Louisville Chamber (502-566-5037)

Area Code 606
The Lane Report (Keven McKew, editor) (606-244-3522; http://laneky.com)

Greater Lexington Chamber (606-252-2559)

Louisiana
Area Code 318
Lafayette Chamber (318-233-2705)
Shreveport Chamber (318-677-2500)

Area Code 504
Baton Rouge Business Report (504-928-1700; http://www.businessreport.com)
Livingston Business Journal (504-665-7744)
New Orleans City Business (504-834-9292; http://www.neworleans.com)

The Freeman Report (an overview of New Orleans public companies, produced by Peter Ricchiuti, associate dean at the Tulane School of Business) (504-862-8489)

Baton Rouge Chamber (504-381-7125)
New Orleans Chamber (504-527-6900)

Maine
Area Code 207
Greater Bangor Business Monthly (207-942-5800)

Maryland
Area Code 410
Baltimore Business Journal (410-263-0715)
Daily Record (410-752-1717)
Harford Business Ledger (410-638-5375)
Washington Business Journal (703-875-2200; http://www.amcity.com/washington)
Washington Technology (703-848-2800; http://www.wtonline.com/wtonline)

Ferris Baker Watts RB (410-685-2600)
Legg Mason Wood Walker RB (410-539-0000)
Wheat First Butcher Singer RB (410-685-8991)

Baltimore-Washington Venture Group c/o Chris Campbell VCC (301-405-2144)

Baltimore County Chamber (410-825-6200)

Massachusetts
Area Code 617
Boston Business Journal (617-330-1000l; http://www.amcity.com.boston)

Technology Capital Network VCC (617-253-7163)

MIT Enterprise Forum of Cambridge c/o Trish Fleming VCC (617-253-8238)
128 Group VCC (617-259-8776)

Greater Boston Chamber (617-253-7163)

Area Code 508
Worcester Business Journal (508-755-8004; http://www.wbjournal.com)

A. G. Edwards RB (508-752-6773)

Worcester Chamber (508-753-2924)

Area Code 413
Berkshire Trade and Commerce (413-447-7700)

Greater Springfield Chamber (413-787-1555)

Michigan
Area Code 313
Crain's Detroit Business (313-446-6000; http://www.crainsdetroit.com)

McDonald & Co. RB (313-665-8500)
Roney & Co. RB (313-963-6700)

Environmental Capital Network VCC (313-996-8387; http://www.bizserve.com/ecn/)
Southeastern Michigan Venture Group

Flint Chamber (313-232-7101)
Hamtramck Chamber (313-875-7877)

Area Code 517
McDonald & Co. RB (517-336-8240)
Roney & Co. RB (517-332-4081)

Detroit Chamber (517-372-2278)
Lansing Regional Chamber (517-487-6340)
Michigan Chamber (517-371-2100)

Area Code 616
Business Update—Grand Rapids (616-281-3800)
Enterprise Business Newspaper—Kalamazoo (616-343-4636)
Grand Rapids Business Journal (616-459-4545)

Hilliard Lyons RB (800-444-1854)
McDonald & Co. RB (616-732-3380)
Roney & Co. RB (616-456-8691)

Travis Bay Enterprise Forum c/o Dick Beldin, Northwest Michigan Council of
   Governments VCC (616-929-5000)

Grand Rapids Chamber (616-459-7221)

Area Code 810
Insider Business Journal (810-220-1800; http://www.insiderbiz.com)

Minnesota
Area Code 507
Mankato Valley Venture Capital Club (507-345-4513)

Area Code 612
Corporate Report Minnesota (612-338-4288)
Minneapolis/St. Paul City Business (612-288-2100; http://www.amcity.com/
   twincities)
Twin Cities Business Monthly (612-339-7571; http://wcco.com/tcbd)

Dain Bosworth RB (612-371-2811)
Piper Jaffray RB (612-342-5800)

Center for Entrepreneurship VCC (612-962-4413)
Minnesota New Venture Collaborative VCC (612-338-3828)

Greater Minneapolis Chamber (612-370-9170)
Minnesota Chamber (612-292-4650)
St. Paul Area Chamber (612-223-5000)

Mississippi
Area Code 601
Mississippi Business Journal (601-364-1000)

J. C. Bradford RB (601-627-2501)
Morgan Keegan RB (601-368-2200; http://www.morgankeegan.com)

Metro Jackson Chamber (601-948-7575)

Missouri
Area Code 816 (Kansas City)
Ingram's magazine (816-842-9994)
Kansas City Business Journal (816-421-5900)

George K. Baum RB (816-474-1100)

Greater Kansas City Chamber (816-221-2424)
South Kansas City Chamber (816-942-4333)

Area Code 314 (St. Louis)
St. Louis Business Journal (314-421-6200)

St. Louis Chamber (314-726-3033)

Area Code 417
Branson Business Journal (417-334-8073)
Springfield Business (417-831-3238)

Area Code 573
Columbia Business Times (573-499-1830)
Mid-Missouri Business (573-443-1311)

Montana
Area Code 406
Big Sky Business Journal (406-259-2309)
Western Business (406-248-7322)

D. A. Davidson RB (406-248-7851)
Dain Bosworth RB (406-252-6306)

Nebraska
Area Code 402
Business Life Omaha (402-558-8909)
Omaha Business Journal (402-330-1760)
Strictly Business (402-432-6245)

Kirkpatrick Pettis RB (402-398-8326)

Nebraska Venture Group c/o University of Nebraska VCC (402-554-8318)

Greater Omaha Chamber (402-346-5000)
Lincoln Chamber (402-476-7511)
Lincoln Women's Chamber (402-488-2034)
Norfolk Chamber (402-371-4862)
Oakland Chamber (402-685-5094)

Nevada
Area Code 702 (Las Vegas)
Las Vegas Business Press (702-871-6780)
Nevada Business Journal (702-735-7003)

Wedbush Morgan Securities RB (702-732-4571)

Las Vegas Chamber (702-735-1616)

New Hampshire
Area Code 603
Business New Hampshire Magazine (603-626-6354)
It's About Business (603-889-8558)
New Hampshire Business Review (603-624-1442)

New Jersey
Area Code 201
Gibraltar Securities RB (201-822-2500)
Hill Thomson RB (201-434-6900)

Venture Association of New Jersey (Morristown) c/o Clara Stricchiola VCC
(201-631-5680)

Paterson Chamber (201-881-7300)

Area Code 609
Janney Montgomery Scott RB (609-231-8400)

New Jersey Technology Council VCC (609-452-1010)

New Jersey State Chamber (609-989-7888)

Area Code 908
Business News-New Jersey (908-246-7677; http://www.bnjol.com)

Wheat First Butcher Singer RB (908-654-6380)

Woodbridge Metro Chamber (908-636-4040)

Area Code 973
Financial Northeastern RB (973-882-9337)
Gibraltar Securities RB (973-822-2500)
Ryan Beck & Co. RB (973-325-3000)

New Mexico
Area Code 505
Albuquerque Business Times (505-880-8370)
Mesilla Valley Business Journal (505-524-6847)
New Mexico Business Weekly (505-768-7008)

Albuquerque Chamber (505-764-3700)
South Valley Chamber (505-873-0551)

New York
Area Codes 212, 718 (New York City)
Crain's New York Business (212-210-0259; http://www.crainsny.com)

New York Venture Group VCC (212-832-6984; http://www.virtual-ny.com/nyvg/)

East Manhattan Chamber (212-831-4206)

Area Code 315 (Syracuse)
CNY Business Journal (315-472-3104)
Syracuse Business (315-472-6911)

Cadaret, Grant & Co. RB (315-471-2191)
Jameson, Dewitt & Associates RB (315-422-1200)
Leigh Baldwin & Co. RB (315-655-2964)

Syracuse Chamber (315-470-1800)

Area Code 518 (Albany)
Capital District Business Review (518-437-9855)

ALVEST Financial Services RB (518-432-2301)
First Albany RB (518-447-8500)
McGinn Smith & Co RB (518-449-5131)
Purshe Kaplan Sterling Investments RB (518-436-3536)

Area Code 716 (Rochester)
Business First of Buffalo (716-882-6200)
Rochester Business Journal (716-546-8303; http://www.rbj.net)

A. G. Edwards & Sons RB (716-271-0300)
Essex Investment Group RB (716-272-2300)
Excel Securities RB (716-424-1234)
H. J. Meyers & Co. RB (716-256-4600)
Pittsford Capital Markets RB (716-385-2700)
Wall Street Financial Group RB (716-442-7560)

Amherst Chamber (716-632-6905)
Rochester Chamber (716-454-2220)

Area Code 914
Fairfield County Business Journal—White Plains (914-694-3600)
Hudson Valley Business Journal (914-258-4007)
Inside Business—Middletown (914-342-2115)
Westchester County Business—White Plains (914-694-3600)

County Chamber—White Plains (914-948-2110)
Tri-State Chamber—Port Jervis (914-856-6694)

Other Area Codes
Long Island Business News (516-737-1700; http://www.libiznews.com)

North Carolina
Area Code 704
Business Journal of Charlotte (704-347-2340)
Business North Carolina (704-523-6987)

Hilliard Lyons RB (800-444-1854)
Interstate Johnson Lane RB (704-379-9000)
J. C. Bradford RB (704-362-8200)
Marion Bass Securities RB (704-523-9407)
Morgan Keegan RB (800-366-7426; http://www.morgankeegan.com)
Wheat First Butcher Singer RB (704-347-5600)

Charlotte Chamber (704-383-3861)

Area Code 910
Business Life (910-812-8801)

Greensboro Chamber (910-275-8675)

Area Code 919
Business Leader (919-872-7077)
Triangle Business Journal (919-878-0010)

Capital Investment Group RB (919-831-2370)
Interstate/Johnson Lane RB (919-881-1000)
J. C. Bradford & Co. RB (919-787-2005)
Marion Bass Securities RB (919-878-5614)
Morgan Keegan RB (800-366-7426; http://www.morgankeegan.com)
Wheat First Butcher Singer RB (919-782-1200)

Council for Entrepreneurial Development VCC (919-544-4642)
North Carolina Investment Network VCC (919-755-5202; http://
ncin.i40.com.ncin)

Durham Chamber (919-682-2133)
Greater Raleigh Chamber (919-664-7000)

North Dakota
Area Code 701
Business Journal—Mandan (701-663-6823)

Minnadak Seed Capital Club VCC (701-777-3132)

Bismarck/Mandan Chamber (701-223-5660)
Carrington Chamber (701-652-2524)

Ohio
Area Codes 216, 330 (Cleveland)
Crain's Cleveland Business (216-522-1383; http://www.crainscleveland.com)
Lake County Business Journal (216-975-9580)

Hilliard Lyons RB (800-444-1854)
McDonald & Co. (216-443-2300)
Ohio Co. RB (216-241-7150)

Ohio Venture Association c/o Debbie Victory at the Akron Regional
Development Board VCC (330-376-5550)

Middleburg Heights Chamber (216-243-5599)
Parma Area Chamber (216-886-1700)

Area Code 513
Cincinnati Business Courier (513-621-6665)

Hilliard Lyons RB (800-444-1854)
Ohio Co. RB (513-651-3000)
Provident Securities RB (513-579-2365)
Ross, Sinclaire and Assoc. RB (513-381-3939)

Greater Cincinnati Venture Association VCC (513-579-3128)

Greater Cincinnati Chamber (513-579-3100)

Area Code 614 (Columbus)
Business First—Columbus (614-461-4040)

228 / Appendix A: Local Sources

Hilliard Lyons RB (800-444-1854)
McDonald & Co. RB (614-228-6292)
Ohio Co. RB (614-464-6880)

Greater Columbus Chamber (614-221-1321; 614-225-6933)
Ohio Chamber (614-228-4201)

Other Area Codes
Dayton Business Reporter (937-291-2386)
Miami Valley Business News (937-222-6900)

Miami Valley Venture Association c/o Karrie Stock VCC (937-228-1141)

Dayton Area Chamber (937-226-1444)

Toledo Business Journal (419-244-8200)

Toledo Area Chamber (419-243-8191)

North Central Business Journal—Orrville (330-682-2055)

Oklahoma
Area Code 405
The Journal Record (405-235-3100)

Capitol Chamber (405-424-4605)
Oklahoma City Chamber (405-297-8900)

Area Code 918
Tulsa Business Journal (918-663-1414)

Oklahoma Investment Forum VCC (918-585-1201)

Greenwood Chamber (918-585-2084)
Metro Tulsa Chamber (918-585-1201)
Oil Capital Chamber (918-663-5464)

Oregon
Area Code 503
Lower Columbia Business—Seaside (503-738-3398)
Marple's Business Newsletter (206-281-9609)
Oregon Business Magazine (503-223-0304)
Red Chip Review (small-cap newsletter based in Portland) (503-241-1265)

Black & Co. RB (503-248-9600)
Charter Investment Group RB (503-223-7711)

Pacific Crest Securities RB (503-248-0721)
Paulson Investment Company RB (503-243-6000)
Wedbush Morgan Securities RB (503-224-0480)

Oregon/MIT Venture Forum VCC (503-227-1111)

Portland Chamber (503-228-9411)

Area Code 541
Business News (541-343-6636; http://www.northwestmedia.com)
Cascade Business News—Bend (541-388-5665)
Marple's Business Newsletter (206-281-9609)
Oregon Business (206-365-9476)

Wedbush Morgan Securities RB (541-485-0202)

Pennsylvania
Area Code 215
Philadelphia Business Journal (215-238-1450; http://www.amcity.com/
  philadelphia)

Janney Montgomery Scott RB (215-665-6000)

Pennsylvania Private Investors Group VCC (215-975-9430)
Philadelphia Venture Group VCC (215-790-3660)

Greater Philadelphia Chamber (215-972-3937)

Area Code 412
Pittsburgh Business Times (412-481-6397)

Allegheny Investments RB (412-367-3880)
Hefren-Tillotson RB (412-343-0990)
Janney Montgomery Scott RB (412-565-3200)
Parker/Hunter RB (412-562-8000)

Enterprise Corporation VCC (412-687-4300)

Pittsburgh Chamber (412-392-4500)

Other Area Codes
Central Pennsylvania Business Journal (717-236-4300)
Eastern Pennsylvania Business Journal (610-398-1026)
Pennsylvania Business Central (814-867-2222)

Rhode Island
Area Code 401
Providence Business News (401-273-2201)

Venture Capital Club of Providence c/o Lauderdale Investment
  Company (401-272-4700)

Greater Providence Chamber (401-521-5000)

South Carolina
Area Code 803
Business Monthly of Greater Columbia (803-731-7794)

Private Investors Network—Aiken VCC (803-648-6851 x3518)

Charleston Metro Chamber (803-577-2510)
Greater Columbia Chamber (803-733-1110)

Area Code 864
Greenville Business Magazine (864-271-1105)
Spartanburg Business Report (864-573-9983)

South Dakota
Area Code 603
Business Page—Sioux Falls (603-336-2218)

Tennessee
Area Code 423
Chattanooga Business Journal (423-629-7500)

J. C. Bradford & Co. RB (423-652-9770)

Chattanooga Chamber (423-756-2121)
Greater Knoxville Chamber (423-637-4550)

Area Code 615
Nashville Business Journal (615-248-2222; http://www.nashbiz.com)

Equitable Securities Corp. RB (615-780-9300)
Hilliard Lyons RB (800-444-1854)
J. C. Bradford RB (800-342-8016)
Morgan Keegan RB (615-255-0600; http://www.morgankeegan.com)
Wiley Brothers RB (615-255-6431)

Nashville Health Care Council (615-460-5660)
Seed Capital Network VCC (615-573-4655)

Nashville Chamber (615-259-4755)

Area Code 901
Memphis Business Journal (901-523-1000)

Bartlett Area Chamber (901-372-9457)

Texas
Area Code 210
Eagle Pass Business Journal (210-757-2705)
Rio Grande Valley Business (210-546-5113)
San Antonio Business Journal (210-341-3202)

Alamo City Chamber (210-226-9055)
Southside Chamber (210-533-5867)
Westside Chamber (210-270-4540)

Area Codes 214, 817 (Dallas/Fort Worth)
Business Press (817-336-8300)
Dallas Business Journal (214-696-5959)
Inside Collin County Business (972-612-2425)
Texas Business Magazine (214-265-7360)

Cullum & Sandow Securities RB (214-754-0111)
Rauscher Pierce Refsnes RB (214-989-1000)
Signal Securities RB (817-877-4256)
Southwest Securities RB (214-651-1800)

Dallas Chamber (214-746-6600)
Fort Worth Chamber (817-336-2491)
Greater Dallas Chamber (214-321-6446)
Plano Chamber (214-424-7547)

Area Code 512
Arriba-Art & Business News (512-479-6397)
Austin Business Journal (512-494-2500; http://www.amcity.com.austin)
Victoria Business Magazine (512-572-3137)

Cullum & Sandow Securities RB (512-328-7774)
Rauscher Pierce & Refsnes RB (512-478-4125)

The Capital Network VCC (512-305-0826; http://thecapitalnetwork.com)

Austin Chamber (512-478-9383)
Capital City Chamber (512-459-1181)

Area Codes 713, 281 (Houston)
Business Today (281-480-5559)
Houston Business Journal (713-688-8811)
Houston Business Review (713-961-9169)

Coastal Securities (713-435-4300)
IMS Securities RB (713-266-2993)
Rauscher Pierce Refsnes RB (713-652-3033)
Texas Capital Securities RB (713-968-7900)

Houston Chamber (713-955-1100)

Other Area Codes
El Paso Chamber (915-534-0500)
Lubbock Chamber (806-763-4666)

Utah
Area Code 801
Business News Advisor (801-674-4727)
Business Source (801-485-3493)

MountainWest Venture Group VCC (801-579-8950)

Salt Lake City Chamber (801-466-3377)

Vermont
Area Code 802
Business Digest South—Burlington (802-862-4109)
Valley Business Journal (802-295-8747)
Vermont Business Magazine (802-863-8038)

Virginia
Area Code 540
Blue Ridge Regional Business Journal (540-985-0143)
North Valley Business Journal—Winchester (540-667-5730)
Quad-State Business Journal—Winchester (540-667-5730)

Area Code 703
Washington Business Journal (703-875-2200; http://www.amcity.com/washington)
Washington Technology (703-848-2800; http://www.wtonline.com)

Ferris Baker Watts RB (703-527-8140)
Legg Mason Wood Walker RB (703-684-0520)
Wheat First Butcher Singer RB (703-739-4500)

American Entrepreneurs for Economic Growth VCC (703-351-5246)
National Venture Capital Association VCC (703-351-5269)

Central Fairfax Chamber (703-591-2450)

Area Code 804
Richmond Ventures Magazine (804-644-1607)
Virginia Business magazine (804-649-6999)

Anderson Strudwick RB (804-643-2400)
Branch Cabell RB (804-225-1400)
Davenport & Co. RB (804-780-2000)
Ferris Baker Watts RB (804-644-7057)
Scott & Stringfellow RB (804-643-1811)
Wheat First Butcher Singer RB (804-649-2311)

Richmond Area Investor Network (RAIN) VCC (804-740-6047)
Richmond Venture Capital Club VCC (804-697-4210)

Greater Richmond Chamber (804-648-1234)
Hampton Roads Chamber (804-622-2312)
Virginia Beach Chamber (804-490-1223)

Washington
Area Code 206
Marple's Business Newsletter (206-281-9609)
Pierce County Business Examiner (206-851-3705)
Puget Sound Business Journal (206-583-0701)
Red Chip Review (small-cap newsletter based in Portland) (503-241-1265)

Dain Bosworth RB (206-621-3111)
Piper Jaffray RB (206-646-7700)

Northwest Venture Group VCC (206-344-3588)
Puget Sound Venture Club VCC (206-344-3588)
Western Investment Network VCC (206 441-3123)

Fife Chamber (206-922-9320)
Greater Seattle Chamber (206-389-7200)
Seattle Chamber (206-461-7200)

Area Code 509
Journal of Business (509-456-5257)
Marple's Business Newsletter (206-281-9609)
Wenatchee Business Journal (509-663-6730)

Spokane Chamber (509-624-1393)
Spokane Valley Chamber (509-924-4994)

Area Code 360
Kitsap Business Journal—Port Richard (360-876-7900)
Marple's Business Newsletter (206-281-9609)
Peninsula Business Journal—Sequim (360-683-3205)
South Sound Business Examiner (360-956-3133)
Vancouver Business Journal (360-695-2442)

Washington, D.C.
Area Code 202
Washington Business Journal (703-875-2200; http://www.amcity.com/washington)
Washington Technology (703-848-2800; http://www.wtonline.com)

Ferris Baker Watts RB (202-429-3500)
Legg Mason Wood Walker (202-452-4000)
Wheat First Butcher Singer RB (202-828-8100)

D.C. Chamber (202-347-7201)

Wisconsin
Area Code 414
Business Journal of Milwaukee (414-278-7788)

Brown Deer Chamber (414-365-9090)
Kenosha Chamber (414-697-1880)

Other Area Codes
Business North—Superior (715-392-1141)

Madison Chamber (608-256-8348)

Wyoming
Area Code 307
Greater Cheyenne Chamber (307-638-3388)

APPENDIX B:
LISTING OF INITIAL
PUBLIC OFFERINGS

The following companies went public in the twelve months ending June 30, 1997. They're presented here for two reasons: first, to give an idea of just how many small public companies are being born out there; and second, to act as a starting point for your local research. Call the firms in your general area and ask for an investor's packet, and you'll have the beginnings of a coverage list.

	City	*Business*	*Telephone*
Alabama			
Hibbett Sporting Goods, Inc.	Birmingham	Sporting goods	205-942-4292
PJ America, Inc.	Birmingham	Restaurants	205-836-1212
Southern Community Bancshares, Inc.	Cullman	Bank	205-734-4863
Arizona			
CRAGAR Industries, Inc.	Phoenix	Wheels and accessories	602-247-1300

	City	Business	Telephone
Poore Brothers, Inc.	Goodyear	Snack-food products	602-925-0731
Rental Service Corp.	Scottsdale	Equipment rental	602-905-3300
SkyMall, Inc.	Phoenix	In-flight catalogs	602-254-9777
Styling Technology Corp.	Phoenix	Hair and skin care	602-263-2362
Ugly Duckling Corporation	Phoenix	Used cars	800-843-3825
Ventana Medical Systems, Inc.	Tucson	Medical instruments	520-887-2155

Arkansas

	City	Business	Telephone
Staffmark, Inc.	Fayetteville	Business staffing	501-973-6000

California

	City	Business	Telephone
ABT Global Pharmaceutical Corp.	Irvine	Pharmaceuticals	714-224-2555
Accelgraphics, Inc.	San Jose	Windows software	408-441-1556
Advanced Aerodynamics & Structures, Inc.	Long Beach	Jet aircraft	310-988-2088
Advanced Fibre Communications, Inc.	Petaluma	Telecommunications	707-794-7700
Affymetrix, Inc.	Santa Clara	Genetic technologies	408-522-6000
Alexandria Real Estate Equities, Inc.	Pasadena	Real estate	213-687-5000

	City	Business	Telephone
Alyn Corp.	Irvine	Industrial products	714-475-1525
American Equity Trust, Inc.	El Segundo	Real estate	310-536-0926
American Materials & Technologies Corp.	Los Angeles	Materials technology	310-841-5200
Applied Imaging Corp.	Santa Clara	Clinical analysis systems	408-562-0250
Aradigm Corp.	Hayward	Drug delivery systems	510-783-0100
Arden Realty Group, Inc.	Beverly Hills	Real estate	310-271-8600
ATL Products, Inc.	Anaheim	Magnetic tape libraries	714-780-7200
Aurora Biosciences Corp.	La Jolla	Drug discovery systems	619-452-5000
Aurum Software, Inc.	Santa Clara	Business software	408-986-8100
Aviation Distributors Inc.	Irvine	Aircraft parts	714-586-7558
Aviron, Inc.	Mountain View	Pharmaceuticals	415-919-6500
Award Software International, Inc.	Mountain View	PC Software	415-968-4433
BA Merchant Services, Inc.	San Francisco	Payment processing	415-241-3390
Bea Systems, Inc.	Sunnyvale	Business software	408-743-4000
Biosite Diagnostics Inc.	San Diego	Diagnostics	619-455-4808
Brilliant Digital Entertainment, Inc.	Woodland Hills	Digital entertainment	818-346-3653

	City	Business	Telephone
BroadVision, Inc.	Los Altos	Internet software	415-943-3600
Cable-Sat Systems, Inc.	San Jose	Facsimile transmission	408-879-6600
Calpine Corp.	San Jose	Power generation	408-995-5115
Calypte Biomedical Corp.	Berkeley	AIDS testing	510-526-2541
Cardiac Pathways Corp.	Sunnyvale	Surgical devices	408-737-0505
Cardima, Inc.	Fremont	Surgical devices	510-354-0300
Cardiovascular Dynamics, Inc.	Irvine	Catheters	714-457-9546
CB Commercial Real Estate Services	Los Angeles	Commercial real estate	213-613-3123
Cellnet Data Systems, Inc.	San Carlos	Wireless communication	415-508-6000
Central Financial Acceptance Corp.	Commerce	Consumer finance	213-720-8600
Channell Commercial Corp.	Temecula	Thermoplastic enclosures	909-694-9160
Chicago Pizza & Brewery, Inc.	Mission Viejo	Restaurants/ breweries	714-367-8616
CN Biosciences, Inc.	San Diego	Pharmaceuticals	619-450-9600
C-Net, Inc.	San Francisco	Technology trade shows	415-395-7800
Connect, Inc.	Mountain View	Internet software	415-254-4000

	City	*Business*	*Telephone*
Cornerstone Propane Partners, L.P.	Watsonville	Propane	408-724-1921
Coulter Pharmaceutical, Inc.	Palo Alto	Pharmaceuticals	415-842-7300
CV Therapeutics, Inc.	Palo Alto	Pharmaceuticals	415-812-0585
CyberMedia, Inc.	Santa Monica	Windows-based software	310-581-4700
Cymer Laser Technologies, Inc.	San Diego	Industrial lasers	619-487-2442
DAOU Systems, Inc.	San Diego	Computer networks	619-452-2221
Diedrich Coffee, Inc.	Irvine	Specialty coffees	714-260-1600
Digital Power Corp.	Fremont	Switching supplies	510-657-2635
Document Sciences Corp.	San Diego	Document software	619-625-2000
E*Trade Group, Inc.	Palo Alto	On-line brokerage	415-842-2500
Earthlink Network Inc.	Pasadena	Internet service provider	818-296-2400
Eco Soil Systems Inc.	San Diego	Industrial microbes	619-675-1660
Farallon Communications, Inc.	Alameda	Internet systems	510-814-5100
Film Roman, Inc.	North Hollywood	Television programming	818-761-2544
First Alliance Mortgage Co.	Irvine	Residential mortgages	714-224-8500

	City	Business	Telephone
First Virtual Holdings Inc.	San Diego	Internet commerce	619-793-2700
Four Media Company	Burbank	Broadcast services	818-840-7000
Fusion Medical Technologies, Inc.	Mountain View	Wound-closure products	415-903-4000
Genesys Telecommunications Laboratories	San Francisco	Business software	415-437-1100
Geron Corp.	Menlo Park	Pharmaceuticals	415-473-7700
Grand Prix Association of Long Beach, Inc.	Long Beach	Motor sports	310-981-2600
Guess ?, Inc.	Los Angeles	Casual clothes	213-765-3100
Guitar Center, Inc.	Agoura Hills	Guitar retailer	818-735-8800
Hambrecht & Quist Group, Inc.	San Francisco	Investment bank	415-576-3300
Healthdesk Corp.	Berkeley	Health-care information	510-883-2160
Heuristic Development Group, Inc.	Pacific Palisades	Exercise advice	310-230-3394
Hot Topic, Inc.	Pomona	Music products	909-869-6373
IA Corp.	Emeryville	Financial software	510-450-7000
Infinity Financial Technology, Inc.	Mountain View	Business software	415-940-6100
Infoseek Corp.	Santa Clara	Web-based information	408-567-2700

	City	Business	Telephone
Ingram Micro, Inc.	Santa Ana	Microcomputer products	714-566-1000
Integrated Surgical Systems, Inc.	Sacramento	Surgical devices	916-646-3487
Intellicell Corp.	Van Nuys	Wireless communications	818-906-7777
Interlink Computer Sciences, Inc.	Fremont	Networking software	510-657-9800
International Network Services, Inc.	Sunnyvale	Networking services	408-542-0100
JetFax, Inc.	Menlo Park	Business software	415-324-0600
Kaynar Technologies, Inc.	Fullerton	Specialty fasteners	714-871-1550
Keystone Automotive Industries, Inc.	Pomona	Auto parts	909-624-8041
Larscom, Inc.	Santa Clara	Networking technologies	408-988-6600
Laser Power Corp.	San Diego	Industrial lasers	619-755-0700
Long Beach Financial Corp.	Orange	Residential mortgages	714-541-5378
Macrovision Corp.	Sunnyvale	Video security	408-743-8600
Maxim Pharmaceuticals, Inc.	San Diego	Pharmaceuticals	619-453-4040
Meade Instruments Corp.	Irvine	Telescopes	714-756-2291
Metrika Systems Corp.	San Diego	On-line industrial services	619-450-9649

	City	Business	Telephone
Micro Therapeutics, Inc.	San Clemente	Medical devices	714-361-0616
Monterey Resources, Inc.	Bakersfield	Oil and gas	805-322-3992
NeoMagic Corp.	Santa Clara	Computer components	408-988-7020
Neotherapeutics, Inc.	Newport Beach	Pharmaceuticals	714-832-4902
North Face, Inc.	San Leandro	Outdoor apparel	510-618-3500
ONSALE, Inc.	Mountain View	On-line commerce	415-428-0600
Overland Data, Inc.	San Diego	Data storage systems	619-571-5555
PacificAmerica Money Center, Inc.	Woodland Hills	Mortgage lending	818-992-8999
Pacific Biometrics, Inc.	Irvine	Diagnostic technologies	714-263-9933
Pacific Coast Apparel Company, Inc.	Culver City	Men's sportswear	310-636-8432
Pacific Gateway Exchange, Inc.	Burlingame	Telecommunications	415-375-6700
Pacific Greystone Corp.	Los Angeles	Homebuilding	213-436-6300
Panavision, Inc.	Woodland Hills	Motion-picture cameras	818-316-1000
PC411, Inc.	Inglewood	On-line directory assistance	310-645-1114
Peerless Systems Corp.	El Segundo	Imaging systems	310-536-0908

	City	Business	Telephone
Peregrine Systems, Inc.	San Diego	Business software	619-481-5000
Pioneer Commercial Funding Corp.	Reseda	Mortgage lender	818-776-0590
Powerwave Technologies, Inc.	Irvine	Radio amplifiers	714-757-0530
Printrak International Inc.	Anaheim	Fingerprint identification	888-321-2347
Procom Technology, Inc.	Irvine	Data storage systems	714-852-1000
Provident Financial Holdings, Inc.	Riverside	Bank holding company	909-686-6060
Puma Technology, Inc.	San Jose	Data-exchange software	408-321-7650
QuadraMed Corp.	Larkspur	Business software	415-461-7725
Qualix Group, Inc.	San Mateo	Business software	415-572-0200
Rambus, Inc.	Mountain View	Microprocessors	415-903-3800
Raster Graphics, Inc.	San Jose	Color-printing systems	408-232-4000
RemedyTemp, Inc.	San Juan Capistrano	Temporary staffing	714-661-1211
Research Engineers, Inc.	Yorba Linda	Engineering software	714-974-2500
Rockshox, Inc.	San Jose	Bicycle products	408-435-7469
Scoop Inc.	Santa Ana	Internet information	714-225-6000

	City	Business	Telephone
SCPIE Holdings, Inc.	Beverly Hills	Malpractice insurance	310-551-5900
Siebel Systems, Inc.	Menlo Park	Business software	415-329-6500
Signature Resorts, Inc.	Los Angeles	Time-share resorts	213-622-2211
Silicon Gaming, Inc.	Palo Alto	Interactive slot machines	415-842-9000
Simulation Sciences Inc.	Brea	Simulation software	714-579-0412
Smartalk Teleservices, Inc.	Los Angeles	Telecommunications	310-444-8800
Solopoint, Inc.	Los Gatos	Consulting	408-364-8850
Sound Source Interactive, Inc.	Westlake Village	Educational software	805-494-9996
Splash Technology Holdings, Inc.	Sunnyvale	Computer equipment	408-328-6300
Star Telecommunications, Inc.	Santa Barbara	Long distance service	805-899-1962
Storage Dimensions, Inc.	Milpitas	Data storage systems	408-954-0710
Storm Technology, Inc.	Mountain View	Digital imaging	415-691-6600
Technology Modeling Associates, Inc.	Sunnyvale	Simulation software	408-328-0930
Thermatrix Inc.	San Jose	Environmental technology	408-453-0490
Thinking Tools, Inc.	Monterey	Simulation software	408-373-8688

	City	Business	Telephone
Ticketmaster Group, Inc.	Los Angeles	Automated ticketing	213-381-2000
Tomorrow's Morning, Inc.	Los Angeles	Children's newspaper	310-440-2778
TriTeal Corp.	Carlsbad	Business software	619-930-2077
Unify Corp.	San Jose	Business software	408-467-4500
Univision Communications, Inc.	Los Angeles	Spanish television	310-556-7600
USCS International, Inc.	Rancho Cordova	Business software	916-636-4500
U.S. Rentals, Inc.	Modesto	Equipment rental	209-544-9000
VDI Media, Inc.	Hollywood	Video duplication	213-957-5500
Verilink Corporation	San Jose	Telecommunications	408-945-1199
Versant Object Technology Corp.	Menlo Park	Database management	415-329-7500
ViaSat, Inc.	Carlsbad	Telecommunications	619-438-8099
Visigenic Software, Inc.	San Mateo	Database software	415-286-1900
Willis Lease Finance Corp.	Sausalito	Aircraft-engine leasing	415-331-5281

Colorado

	City	Business	Telephone
Abacus Direct Corp.	Westminster	Direct marketing	303-657-2800

	City	Business	Telephone
Accelr8 Technology Corp.	Denver	Business software	303-863-8088
Amerivest Properties, Inc.	Arvada	Real estate	303-421-1224
Einstein/Noah Bagel Corp.	Golden	Bagel stores	303-202-9300
Electroscope, Inc.	Boulder	Surgical equipment	303-444-2600
Global Med Technologies, Inc.	Lakewood	Business software	303-238-2000
Granite Financial, Inc.	Westminster	Equipment leasing	303-650-4059
Image Guided Technologies, Inc.	Boulder	Graphics technologies	303-447-0248
Imagematrix Corp.	Denver	Health-care software	303-399-3700
MarkWest Hydrocarbon, Inc.	Englewood	Natural gas processing	303-290-8700
Matrix Capital Corporation	Denver	Financial services	303-595-9898
MetroGolf, Inc.	Denver	Golf centers	303-294-9300
MoneyGram Payment Systems, Inc.	Lakewood	Wire transfer services	303-716-6800
Navidec, Inc.	Englewood	Internet services	303-790-7565
New Era of Networks, Inc.	Englewood	Business software	303-694-3933
Nhancement Technologies, Inc.	Golden	Voice processing systems	303-271-0505
Optika Imaging Systems, Inc.	Colorado Springs	Business software	719-548-9800

	City	*Business*	*Telephone*
Premier Concepts, Inc.	Aurora	Fake jewelry	303-338-1800
Racom Systems, Inc.	Greenwood Village	Electronic commerce	303-771-2077
Rocky Ford Financial, Inc.	Rocky Ford	Savings and loan	714-254-7642
Rocky Mountain Internet, Inc.	Denver	Internet access provider	303-672-0700
Spatial Technology Inc.	Boulder	Imaging software	303-449-0649
Specialty Care Network, Inc.	Lakewood	Physician practice mgmt.	303-716-0041
Startek, Inc.	Denver	Outsourcing services	303-361-6000
Teletech Holdings, Inc.	Denver	Customer-care services	303-894-4000
Titanium Metals Corp.	Denver	Titanium products	303-296-5600
Vail Resorts, Inc.	Vail	Mountain resorts	970-476-5601
Wild Oats Market, Inc.	Boulder	Natural foods	303-440-5220

Connecticut

Accent Color Sciences, Inc.	East Hartford	Color printers	860-610-4000
Factset Research Systems Inc.	Greenwich	On-line database	203-863-1500
Farmstead Telephone Group, Inc.	East Hartford	Used AT&T telephones	860-282-0010
Fine Host Corp.	Greenwich	Food service	203-629-4320

	City	Business	Telephone
First Aviation Services, Inc.	Stamford	Aircraft services	203-359-7733
Genesee & Wyoming Inc.	Greenwich	Short-line railroads	203-629-3722
Hartford Life, Inc.	Simsbury	Insurance	860-843-7716
International Telecommunications Data	Stamford	Business software	203-329-3300
Lexington Healthcare Group Inc.	New Britain	Nursing homes	860-223-6902
Marine Management Systems, Inc.	Stamford	Shipping software	203-327-6404
MemberWorks Inc.	Stamford	Membership services	203-324-7635
Millbrook Press Inc.	Brookfield	Children's books	203-740-2220
Silgan Holdings, Inc.	Stamford	Packaging products	203-975-7110
Transact Technologies, Inc.	Wallingford	Printers	203-949-9933
Trex Medical Corp.	Danbury	Mammography	203-790-1188
United Natural Foods, Inc.	Dayville	Natural foods	860-779-2800

Delaware

Dover Downs Entertainment, Inc.	Dover	Auto racing	302-674-4600

Florida

Advanced Electronic Support Products, Inc.	North Miami	Computer connectivity	305-944-7710

	City	Business	Telephone
Andean Development Corp.	Boca Raton	Chilean holding company	407-482-6336
Andrx Corp.	Fort Lauderdale	Pharmaceuticals	954-584-0300
Aviation Sales Co.	Miami	Aircraft spare parts	305-592-4055
Capital Factors Holding, Inc.	Fort Lauderdale	Financial services	305-730-2900
Caribbean Cigar Company	Miami	Cigars	305-267-6026
Coast Dental Services, Inc.	Clearwater	Dentistry	813-726-5152
Commodore Holdings Ltd.	Hollywood	Cruise ships	954-967-2100
Conserver Corporation of America	Coral Gables	Industrial products	305-444-3888
Consolidated Cigar Holdings, Inc.	Fort Lauderdale	Cigars	954-772-9000
Digital Lightwave, Inc	Clearwater	Computer systems	813-442-6677
Ensec International, Inc.	Boca Raton	Security systems	561-997-2511
EPIC Insurance Group, Inc.	Jacksonville	Malpractice insurance	904-354-5910
Florida Panthers Holdings, Inc.	Fort Lauderdale	Professional sports	954-768-1900
Frost Hanna Capital Group, Inc.	Boca Raton	Merger vehicle	407-367-1079
Golden Bear Golf, Inc.	North Palm Beach	Golf products	407-626-3900

	City	Business	Telephone
Group Long Distance, Inc.	Fort Lauderdale	Long distance service	954-771-9696
Hamilton Bancorp Inc.	Miami	Bank holding company	305-717-5613
HomeSide, Inc.	Jacksonville	Residential mortgages	904-281-3000
H.T.E., Inc.	Orlando	Public-sector software	407-841-3235
Hvide Marine Inc.	Fort Lauderdale	Marine transportation	954-523-2200
IMC Mortgage Co.	Tampa	Home equity loans	813-932-2211
Information Management Resources, Inc.	Clearwater	Business software	813-797-7080
Innopet Brands Corp.	Fort Lauderdale	Dog food	954-356-0036
Interaction Media Corp.	Coral Gables	Interactive multimedia	305-446-5900
International Speedway Corp.	Daytona Beach	Motorsports	904-254-2700
Kos Pharmaceuticals, Inc.	Miami	Pharmaceuticals	305-577-3464
Mansur Industries, Inc.	Miami	Industrial parts washers	305-232-6768
Medical Manager Corp.	Tampa	Practice management	813-287-2990
Metropolitan Health Networks, Inc.	Boca Raton	Managed health care	561-416-9487
National Auto Finance Co., Inc.	Boca Raton	Vehicle loans	561-997-2747

	City	Business	Telephone
NetSpeak Corp.	Boca Raton	Communications software	561-997-4001
Ocurest Laboratories, Inc.	Palm Beach Gardens	Health care products	561-627-8121
Ocwen Asset Investment Corp.	West Palm Beach	Real estate	561-681-8500
Ocwen Financial Corp.	West Palm Beach	Mortgage lending	561-681-8000
Phoenix International Ltd., Inc.	Maitland	Banking software	407-667-0033
Precision Response Corp.	Miami	Telemarketing	305-626-4600
Preferred Employers Holdings, Inc.	Miami	Insurance	305-893-4040
ProSource, Inc.	Coral Gables	Food service	305-529-2500
Q.E.P. Company, Inc.	Boca Raton	Specialty tools	561-994-5550
Roadhouse Grill, Inc.	Fort Lauderdale	Restaurants	954-489-9699
Sterile Recoveries, Inc.	Clearwater	Surgical products	813-726-4421
Streicher Mobile Fueling, Inc.	Fort Lauderdale	Mobile fueling services	954-739-3880
Summit Holding Southeast, Inc.	Lakeland	Managed health care	941-665-6060
Sun Hydraulics Inc.	Sarasota	Hydraulic cartridge valves	941-362-1200
Swisher International Group, Inc.	Jacksonville	Cigars	904-353-4311

	City	Business	Telephone
Thermacell Technologies, Inc.	New Port Richey	Insulating materials	813-938-3269
2Connect Express, Inc.	Plantation	Communications services	954-797-7960
U.S. Energy Systems, Inc.	West Palm Beach	Power generation	561-820-9779
Vistana, Inc.	Orlando	Time-share resorts	407-239-3000
Vitech America, Inc.	Miami	Computer equipment	305-477-1161
Xomed Surgical Products, Inc.	Jacksonville	Surgical products	904-296-9600

Georgia

	City	Business	Telephone
AHL Services, Inc.	Atlanta	Contract staffing	404-267-2222
Carson, Inc.	Savannah	Ethnic hair care	912-651-3400
Cox Radio, Inc.	Atlanta	Radio broadcasting	404-843-5000
Firearms Training Systems, Inc.	Suwanee	Small arms training	770-813-0180
Gulfstream Aerospace Corp.	Savannah	Business jets	912-965-3000
International Computex, Inc.	Atlanta	Manufacturing software	770-953-1464
Laminating Technologies, Inc.	Canton	Packaging products	404-355-7681
LHS Group, Inc.	Atlanta	Customer management	770-280-3004

	City	Business	Telephone
Medirisk, Inc.	Atlanta	Database software	404-364-6700
Mego Mortgage Corp.	Atlanta	Consumer finance	770-952-6700
Melita International Corp.	Norcross	Customer management	770-239-4000
Physicians' Specialty Corp.	Atlanta	Practice management	404-256-7535
Radiant Systems, Inc.	Alpharetta	Retailing technology	770-772-3000
Security Capital Atlantic, Inc.	Atlanta	Real estate	404-237-9292
Synthetic Industries, Inc.	Chicka-mauga	Polypropylene fabrics	706-375-3121
U.S. Franchise Systems, Inc.	Atlanta	Franchising	404-321-4045

Hawaii

	City	Business	Telephone
Hawaiian Natural Water Company, Inc.	Honolulu	Spring water	808-832-4550

Idaho

	City	Business	Telephone
Coldwater Creek Inc.	Sandpoint	Direct-mail retailing	208-263-2266

Illinois

	City	Business	Telephone
American Disposal Services, Inc.	Burr Ridge	Solid-waste disposal	708-655-1105
American Medserve Corp.	Naperville	Pharmacy services	630-717-2904
Beverly Bancorporation, Inc.	Chicago	Bank holding company	312-881-2214

	City	Business	Telephone
Big Foot Financial Corp.	Long Grove	Bank holding company	847-634-2100
Brookdale Living Communities, Inc.	Chicago	Assisted living	312-456-0239
CCC Information Services Group, Inc.	Chicago	Claims processing	312-222-4636
Diamond Home Services, Inc.	Woodstock	Home improvement	815-334-1414
Diamond Technology Partners Inc.	Chicago	Management consulting	312-255-5000
Dominick's Supermarkets, Inc.	Northlake	Supermarkets	708-562-1000
Donnelley Enterprise Solutions, Inc.	Chicago	Information management	312-419-7660
EVEREN Capital Corp.	Chicago	Brokerage	312-574-6000
First Enterprise Financial Group, Inc.	Evanston	Auto loans	847-866-8665
Home Bancorp of Elgin, Inc.	Elgin	Savings and loan	847-742-3800
Leap Group, Inc.	Chicago	Marketing	312-494-0300
Metromail Corp.	Lombard	Marketing information	708-620-3300
Metzler Group, Inc.	Deerfield	Utility consulting	847-945-0001
Midway Games, Inc.	Chicago	Real estate	630-368-2900
Peapod, Inc.	Evanston	On-line grocery shopping	847-492-8900
PS Financial, Inc.	Chicago	Savings and loan	312-376-3800

	City	Business	Telephone
Racing Champions Corp.	Glen Ellyn	Vehicle replicas	630-790-3507
Ryerson Tull, Inc.	Chicago	Metals processing	312-762-2121
Sabratek Corp.	Niles	Medical devices	847-647-2760
Stericycle, Inc.	Deerfield	Medical-waste disposal	847-945-6550
Total Control Products, Inc.	Melrose Park	Industrial automation	708-345-5500
Universal Outdoor Holdings, Inc.	Chicago	Outdoor advertising	312-644-8673
Vita Food Products, Inc.	Chicago	Specialty foods	312-738-4500
Wesley Jessen Vision Care, Inc.	Des Plaines	Contact lenses	847-294-3000

Indiana

	City	Business	Telephone
DePuy, Inc.	Warsaw	Orthopedic devices	219-267-8143
Essex International, Inc.	Fort Wayne	Copper wire	219-461-4000
River Valley Bancorp, Inc.	Madison	Bank holding company	812-273-4949
St. Joseph Capital Corp.	South Bend	Bank holding company	219-283-0773
Steel Dynamics, Inc.	Butler	Steel minimill	219-868-8000
Steinway Musical Instruments, Inc.	Elkhart	Pianos	219-522-1675
Symons International Group, Inc.	Indianapolis	Insurance	317-259-6300

	City	Business	Telephone
Iowa			
AmerUs Life Holdings, Inc.	Des Moines	Life insurance	515-280-1331
FBL Financial Group, Inc.	Des Moines	Insurance	515-225-5410
McLeod, Inc.	Cedar Rapids	Telecommuni-cations	319-364-0000
Murdock Communications Corp.	Cedar Rapids	Telecommuni-cations	319-362-6900
National Propane Partners, L.P.	Cedar Rapids	Propane	319-365-1550
Smithway Motor Xpress Corp.	Fort Dodge	Truck trans-port	515-576-7418
Kansas			
Candlewood Hotel Co., Inc.	Wichita	Extended-stay hotels	316-631-1300
Electronic Processing, Inc.	Kansas City	Business software	913-321-6392
Gold Banc Corporation, Inc.	Leawood	Bank holding company	913-451-8050
Integrated Medical Resources, Inc.	Lenexa	Medical services	913-894-0591
New York Bagel Enterprises, Inc.	Wichita	Bagel restaurants	316-267-7373
Kentucky			
Arm Financial Group, Inc.	Louisville	Financial services	502-582-7900
Atria Communities, Inc.	Louisville	Assisted living	502-596-7540
Cumberland Mountain Bancshares, Inc.	Middles-boro	Bank holding company	606-248-4584

	City	Business	Telephone
General Cable Corp.	Highland Heights	Copper wire	606-572-8000
Healthcare Recoveries, Inc.	Louisville	Health insurance	502-454-1340
National Processing, Inc.	Louisville	Transaction processing	502-364-2000

Louisiana

First Allen Parish Bancorp	Oakdale	Savings and loan	318-335-2031
GS Financial, Inc.	Metairie	Bank holding company	504-457-6220
Gulf Island Fabrication, Inc.	Houma	Offshore drilling	504-872-2100
Lamar Advertising Company	Baton Rouge	Outdoor advertising	504-926-1000
Rankin Automotive Group, Inc.	Alexandria	Auto parts	318-487-1081

Maine

Brunswick Technologies, Inc.	Brunswick	Composite materials	207-729-7792
Control Devices, Inc.	Standish	Electronic equipment	207-642-4535

Maryland

Ace*Comm Corp.	Gaithersburg	Telecommunications	301-258-9850
CBES Bancorp, Inc.	Excelsior Springs	Bank holding company	816-630-6711
Ciena Corp.	Savage	Telecommunications	301-317-5800

	City	Business	Telephone
Credit Management Solutions, Inc.	Columbia	Business software	410-740-1000
DIGEX, Inc.	Beltsville	Internet service provider	301-847-5000
e-Net, Inc.	Gaithersburg	Internet commerce	301-548-8880
EntreMed, Inc.	Rockville	Blood technologies	301-217-9858
First Mariner Bancorp	Baltimore	Bank holding company	410-342-2600
Healthcare Financial Partners, Inc.	Chevy Chase	Health-care financing	301-961-1640
Integrated Living Communities, Inc.	Owings Mills	Assisted living	410-998-8425
RWD Technologies, Inc.	Columbia	Business technology	410-730-4377
Snyder Communications, Inc.	Bethesda	Marketing services	301-571-1236
Trusted Information Systems, Inc.	Glenwood	Computer security	301-854-6889
United Payors & United Providers, Inc.	Rockville	Health-care management	301-548-1000
V-ONE Corporation	Rockville	Network security products	301-838-8900
Yurie Systems Inc.	Latham	Telecommunications	301-352-4600

Massachusetts

ArQule, Inc.	Medford	Pharmaceuticals	617-395-4100

	City	Business	Telephone
Ascent Pediatrics, Inc.	Wilmington	Pharmaceuticals	508-658-2500
Augment Systems, Inc.	Westford	Information management	508-392-8626
Aware, Inc.	Bedford	Telecommunications	617-276-4000
Bitstream, Inc.	Cambridge	Information software	617-497-6222
Boston Biomedica, Inc.	West Bridgewater	Diagnostic devices	508-580-1900
Boston Communications Group, Inc.	Boston	Customer support	617-476-3570
Cambridge Heart, Inc.	Bedford	Cardiac disease diagnosis	617-271-1200
Cubist Pharmaceuticals, Inc.	Cambridge	Pharmaceuticals	617-576-1999
EPIX Medical, Inc.	Cambridge	Imaging	617-499-1400
Firstfed America Bancorp, Inc.	Fall River	Bank holding company	508-679-8181
Forrester Research, Inc.	Cambridge	Consulting	617-497-7090
GeoTel Communications Corp.	Littleton	Telecommunications	508-486-1100
Harborside Healthcare Corp.	Boston	Long-term health care	617-556-1515
Innovasive Devices, Inc.	Marlborough	Tissue repair systems	508-460-8229
Lightbridge, Inc.	Waltham	Telecommunications	617-890-2000

	City	Business	Telephone
Nexar Technologies, Inc.	Westborough	Personal computers	508-836-8700
Nitinol Medical Technologies, Inc.	Boston	Medical devices	617-737-0930
Object Design, Inc.	Burlington	Internet software	617-674-5000
OneWave, Inc.	Watertown	Internet software	617-923-6500
Pegasystems Inc.	Cambridge	Business software	617-374-9600
Photoelectron Corp.	Lexington	Cancer treatment	617-861-2069
QC Optics, Inc.	Burlington	Industrial lasers	617-272-4949
Registry, Inc.	Newton	Consulting	617-527-6886
Restrac, Inc.	Dedham	Business software	617-320-5600
Seachange International, Inc.	Maynard	Telecommunications	508-897-0100
Selfcare, Inc.	Waltham	Manufacturing	617-647-3900
Specialty Catalog Corp.	South Easton	Direct marketing	508-238-0199
Suburban Ostomy Supply Co., Inc.	Holliston	Medical supplies	508-429-1000
Thermo Fibergen, Inc.	Bedford	Pulp and paper	617-622-1000
Thermo Optek Corp.	Franklin	Analytical instruments	508-528-0551
Transkaryotic Therapies, Inc.	Cambridge	Biotechnology	617-349-0200

	City	Business	Telephone
Virus Research Institute, Inc.	Cambridge	Vaccine delivery	617-864-6232
Visage Technology, Inc.	Acton	Identification systems	508-263-8365
Vivid Technologies, Inc.	Woburn	Baggage inspection	617-938-7800
WebSecure, Inc.	Saugas	Internet services	617-867-2300
Xionics Document Technologies, Inc.	Burlington	Imaging technology	617-229-7000

Michigan

	City	Business	Telephone
Aastrom Biosciences Inc.	Ann Arbor	Cell therapy	313-930-5555
Community Central Bank Corp.	Mount Clemmens	Bank holding company	810-783-4500
Complete Business Solutions, Inc.	Farmington Hills	Business services	810-488-2088
Flagstar Bancorp, Inc.	Bloomfield Hills	Thrift holding company	810-338-7700
Lason, Inc.	Troy	Outsourcing services	810-597-5800
Michigan Brewery, Inc.	Gaylord	Microbrewery/ restaurants	517-731-0401
Riviera Tool Company	Grand Rapids	Metal stamping	616-698-2100
Rofin-Sinar Technologies, Inc.	Plymouth	Industrial lasers	313-455-5400
Superior Consultant Holdings Corp.	Farmington Hills	Health-care consulting	810-855-0960

	City	Business	Telephone
Minnesota			
ACI Telecentrics, Inc.	Minneapolis	Telemarketing	612-928-4700
Dura Automotive Systems, Inc.	Minneapolis	Auto parts	612-332-2335
Endocardial Solutions, Inc.	St. Paul	Coronary diagnosis	612-644-7890
Famous Dave's of America, Inc.	Plymouth	Barbecue restaurants	612-557-5798
Fieldworks, Inc.	Eden Prairie	Portable computers	612-947-0856
Integ, Inc.	St. Paul	Glucose monitoring	612-639-8816
Medi-Ject Corp.	Minneapolis	Injection systems	612-553-1102
Mercury Waste Solutions, Inc.	St. Paul	Hazardous-waste disposal	612-635-0080
Metris Companies, Inc.	St. Louis Park	Consumer credit products	612-525-5020
Nutrition Medical, Inc.	Buffalo	Nutritional products	612-682-9288
Ontrack Data International, Inc.	Eden Prairie	Data recovery services	612-937-1107
Printware, Inc.	St. Paul	Offset printing	612-456-1400
SAC Technologies, Inc.	Edina	Fingerprint identification	612-835-7080
Wilsons, The Leather Experts, Inc.	Brooklyn Park	Leather outerwear	612-391-4000
XOX Corp.	St. Paul	Geometric computing	612-645-9000

	City	*Business*	*Telephone*
Mississippi			
Cal-Maine Foods, Inc.	Jackson	Eggs	601-948-6813
Halter Marine Group, Inc.	Gulfport	Ship building	601-896-0029
Missouri			
Intensiva Healthcare Corp.	St. Louis	Long-term health care	314-725-0112
TALX Corp.	St. Louis	Communications	314-434-0046
Montana			
Empire Federal Bancorp, Inc.	Livingston	Bank holding company	406-222-1981
Nebraska			
AmeriTrade Holding Corp.	Omaha	Discount brokerage	402-331-7856
Transcrypt International, Inc.	Lincoln	Information security	402-474-4800
West Teleser Services Corp.	Omaha	Telecommunications	402-571-7700
Nevada			
Borealis Technology Corp.	Incline Village	Sales automation	702-832-0300
New Hampshire			
Diatide, Inc.	Londonderry	Pharmaceuticals	603-437-8970
White Pine Software, Inc.	Nashua	Connectivity software	603-886-9050

	City	Business	Telephone
New Jersey			
Algos Pharamceuticals Corp.	Neptune	Pain management	908-938-5959
All American Food Group, Inc.	Fairfield	Bagel stores	201-244-9336
All Communications Corp.	Mountain-side	Videoconfer-encing	908-789-8800
Amplidyne, Inc.	Somerset	Power amplifi-ers	908-271-8473
Chem International, Inc.	Hillside	Nutritional supplements	201-926-0816
Debt Strategies Fund, Inc.	Plainsboro	Closed-end fund	609-282-2800
EMCORE Corp.	Somerset	Semiconductor materials	908-271-9090
EP MedSystems, Inc.	Budd Lake	Surgical devices	201-691-6400
FaxSav Inc.	Edison	Facsimile transmission	908-906-2000
Hertz Corp.	Park Ridge	Car rental	201-307-2000
Humascan, Inc.	Cranford	Cancer diagno-sis	908-709-3434
Integrated Technology USA, Inc.	Teaneck	Internet soft-ware	201-907-0200
Intelligroup, Inc.	Iselin	Information technology	908-750-1600
International Sports Wagering, Inc.	Little Falls	Sports betting	201-256-8181
inTest Corp.	Cherry Hill	Semiconductor equipment	609-424-6886

	City	Business	Telephone
Journal Register Company	Trenton	Newspaper publishing	609-396-2200
Linens 'n' Things, Inc.	Clifton	Home textiles	201-778-1300
Medjet, Inc.	Edison	Surgical devices	908-738-3990
Nuwave Technologies, Inc.	Fairfield	Digital imaging	201-882-8810
ObjectSoft Corp.	Hackensack	Transaction software	201-343-9100
Room Plus, Inc.	Paterson	Furniture	201-523-4600
Tellurian, Inc.	Upper Saddle River	Virtual reality	201-818-6767
Translation Group Ltd.	Pennsauken	Language translation	609-663-8600
Voxware, Inc.	Princeton	Digital speech processing	609-514-4100
Worldwide Entertainment & Sports, Inc.	West Orange	Celebrity marketing	201-325-3244

New Mexico

	City	Business	Telephone
Bowlin Outdoor Advertising & Travel	Albuquerque	Travel centers	505-266-5985
Thermo BioAnalysis Corp.	Santa Fe	Biochemical devices	505-471-3232

New York

	City	Business	Telephone
Advanced Health Corp.	Tarrytown	Physician practice mgmt.	914-332-6688

	City	Business	Telephone
Afsala Bancorp, Inc.	Amsterdam	Bank holding company	518-842-5700
American Craft Brewing International	New York	International breweries	212-664-1666
Amertranz Worldwide Holding Corp.	Lake Success	Freight forwarding	516-326-9000
Amscan Holdings, Inc.	Elmsford	Party goods	914-345-2020
ASD Group, Inc.	Poughkeepsie	Manufacturing	914-452-3000
ASI Solutions, Inc.	New York	Human resources	212-319-8400
Baltia Air Lines, Inc.	Jamaica	Air transport	718-553-6636
Bank United Corp.	Uniondale	Bank holding company	516-745-6644
Brylane, Inc.	New York	Catalog retailing	212-613-9500
Cable & Co. Worldwide, Inc.	New York	Men's footwear	212-489-9686
Cadus Pharmaceutical Corp.	Tarrytown	Pharmaceuticals	914-345-3344
Coinmach Laundry Corp.	Roslyn	Laundry equipment	212-278-1509
Commodore Applied Technologies, Inc.	New York	Environmental technology	212-308-5800
Commodore Separation Technologies, Inc.	New York	Separation technology	212-308-5800
Compositech Ltd.	Hauppauge	Semiconductor materials	516-436-5200
Compu-DAWN, Inc.	Cedarhurst	Law enforcement	516-374-6700

	City	Business	Telephone
Cornerstone Properties, Inc.	New York	Real estate	212-605-7100
Decor Group, Inc.	Mount Vernon	Sculptures	914-665-5400
dELiA*s, Inc.	New York	Direct marketing	212-807-9060
Delta Financial Corp.	Woodbury	Consumer finance	516-364-8500
Donna Karan International Inc.	New York	Fashion design	212-789-1500
Ecomat, Inc.	Mamaroneck	Clothing services	914-777-3600
Enamelon, Inc.	Yonkers	Oral hygiene products	914-237-1308
Farm Family Holdings, Inc.	Glenmont	Insurance	518-431-5000
Fun Tyme Concepts, Inc.	Staten Island	Children's entertainment	718-761-6100
General Bearing Corp.	West Nyack	Ball bearings	914-358-6000
General Cigar Holdings, Inc.	New York	Cigars	212-448-3800
General Credit Corp.	New York	Payroll services	212-861-2867
GKN Holding Corp.	New York	Securities brokerage	212-509-3800
Harmat Organization, Inc.	Quogue	Real estate development	516-653-3303
Hertz Technology Group, Inc.	New York	Microcomputers	212-684-4141
Imatec Ltd.	New York	Image processing	212-826-0440
Jenna Lane, Inc.	New York	Sportswear for women	212-704-0002

	City	Business	Telephone
Kapson Senior Quarters Corp.	Woodbury	Assisted living	516-921-8900
Kideo Productions, Inc.	New York	Personalized videos	212-505-6605
K2 Design, Inc.	New York	Web sites	212-614-0191
Leading Edge Packaging, Inc.	New York	Packaging products	212-239-1865
Manchester Equipment Co., Inc.	Hauppauge	Systems integration	516-435-1199
Marquee Group, Inc.	New York	Sports entertainment	212-407-9130
Medialink Worldwide Inc.	New York	Video and audio	212-682-8300
MIM Corp.	Pearl River	Pharmacy management	914-735-3555
ML Direct, Inc.	New York	Infomercials	212-572-6209
Morgan Stanley Russia & New Europe Fund	New York	Closed-end mutual fund	212-296-7100
NAM Corp.	Great Neck	Dispute resolution	516-829-4343
Netlive Communications, Inc.	New York	Video entertainment	212-343-7082
Netsmart Technologies, Inc.	Islip	Business software	516-968-2000
New York Health Care, Inc.	Brooklyn	Home health care	718-421-0500
Orion Acquisition Corp. II	New York	Merger vehicle	212-391-1392
Paradise Music & Entertainment, Inc.	New York	Musical entertainment	212-957-9393

	City	Business	Telephone
Patient Infosystems, Inc.	Rochester	Health-care information	716-242-7200
Pivot Rules, Inc.	New York	Golf sports-wear	212-944-8000
Polo Ralph Lauren Corp.	New York	Clothing	212-318-7000
Puro Water Group, Inc.	Maspeth	Purified drink-ing water	718-326-7000
Roslyn Bancorp, Inc.	Roslyn	Bank holding company	516-621-6000
Special Metals Corp.	New Hart-ford	Alloy products	315-798-2900
Superior Supplements, Inc.	Hauppauge	Dietary supple-ments	516-231-0783
Superior TeleCom Inc.	New York	Copper wire and cable	212-757-3333
Surge Components, Inc.	Deer Park	Electronic products	516-595-1818
SysComm International Corp.	Hauppauge	Systems inte-gration	516-273-3200
Take Two Interactive Software, Inc.	New York	Computer games	212-941-2988
Teleport Communications Group Inc.	Staten Is-land	Local phone service	718-355-2000
Think New Ideas, Inc.	New York	Marketing	212-629-6800
TMP Worldwide, Inc.	New York	Advertising	212-977-4200
TwinLab Corp.	Ronkon-koma	Nutritional supplements	516-467-3140
United Auto Group, Inc.	New York	Automobile dealerships	212-223-3300

	City	Business	Telephone
Unity First Acquisition Corp.	New York	Merger vehicle	212-696-4282
Univec, Inc.	Garden City	Hypodermic syringes	516-294-1000
Viatel, Inc.	New York	Long distance service	212-935-6800
Visual Edge Systems, Inc.	New York	Golf instruction	212-765-1284

North Carolina

Applied Analytical Industries, Inc.	Wilmington	Pharmaceuticals	910-392-1606
Carolina Fincorp, Inc.	Rockingham	Bank holding company	910-997-6245
Century Bancorp, Inc.	Thomasville	Savings and loan	910-475-4663
Newsouth Bancorp, Inc.	Washington	Bank holding company	919-946-4178
Pluma, Inc.	Eden Prairie	Fleece active wear	910-635-4000
RF Micro Devices, Inc.	Greensboro	Wireless communications	910-664-1233
Ridgeview, Inc.	Newton	Sports socks	704-464-2972
South Street Financial Corp.	Albemarle	Bank holding company	704-982-9184
Triangle Pharmaceuticals, Inc.	Durham	Pharmaceuticals	919-493-5980
Tri-Point Medical Corp.	Raleigh	Medical adhesives	919-876-7800

	City	Business	Telephone
Waste Industries, Inc.	Raleigh	Waste disposal	919-782-0095
Wheels Sports Group, Inc.	Mocksville	Sports trading cards	704-634-3000

North Dakota

	City	Business	Telephone
Great Plains Software, Inc.	Fargo	Business software	701-281-0550
RDO Equipment Co.	Fargo	John Deere stores	701-237-6062

Ohio

	City	Business	Telephone
Bigmar, Inc.	Columbus	Infusion solutions	614-848-8380
Boykin Lodging Co.	Cleveland	Real estate	216-241-6375
Ciao Cucina Corp.	Cincinnati	Italian restaurants	513-241-9161
Collaborative Clinical Research, Inc.	Cleveland	Clinical research sites	216-491-9930
Dayton Superior Corp.	Miamisburg	Construction materials	513-866-0711
DeCrane Aircraft Holdings, Inc.	Copley	Avionics components	330-668-3061
Gradall Industries, Inc.	New Philadelphia	Hydraulic excavators	330-339-2211
Lenox Bancorp, Inc.	St. Bernard	Savings and loan	513-242-6900
Market Financial Corp.	Mount Healthy	Savings and loan	513-521-9772
Mazel Stores, Inc.	Solon	Closeout stores	216-248-5200

	City	Business	Telephone
Metropolitan Financial Corp.	Mayfield Heights	Bank holding company	216-646-1111
Miami Computer Supply Corp.	Dayton	Computer equipment	937-429-5211
O'Gara Co.	Fairfield	Vehicle armoring systems	614-848-3995
Peoples Financial Corp.	Massillon	Bank holding company	303-832-7441
Peoples-Sidney Financial Corp.	Sidney	Savings and loan	937-492-6129
Thermo Opportunity Fund, Inc.	Cincinnati	Closed-end mutual fund	800-320-2212

Oklahoma

Applied Intelligence Group, Inc.	Edmond	Information services	405-936-2300
CD Warehouse, Inc.	Oklahoma City	"CD warehouse" stores	405-232-2797
Heritage Propane Partners L.P.	Tulsa	Propane	918-492-7272

Oregon

Antivirals Inc.	Portland	Genetic research	503-227-0554
Claremont Technology Group, Inc.	Beaverton	Information services	503-690-4000
Coffee People, Inc.	Portland	Coffee	503-223-7714
Lithia Motors, Inc.	Medford	Auto retailing	541-776-6899

	City	Business	Telephone
Metro One Telecommunications, Inc.	Beaverton	Wireless information	503-643-9500
Obie Media Corp.	Eugene	Outdoor advertising	541-686-8400
Rogue Wave Software, Inc.	Corvallis	Object-oriented software	541-754-3010
Southern Pacific Funding Corp.	Lake Oswego	Mortgage lending	503-684-4700
Summit Design, Inc.	Beaverton	Software	503-643-9281
Wilshire Financial Services Group, Inc.	Portland	Financial services	503-223-5600

Pennsylvania

	City	Business	Telephone
ANSYS, Inc.	Houston	Business software	412-746-3304
Bionx Implants, Inc.	Malvern	Polymer implants	610-296-0919
CFM Technologies, Inc.	West Chester	Semiconductors	610-696-8300
CollaGenex Pharmaceuticals, Inc.	Newtown	Medical research	215-579-7388
Education Management Corp.	Pittsburgh	Post-secondary education	412-562-0900
Emclaire Financial Corp.	Emlenton	Bank holding company	412-867-2311
First Carnegie Deposit	Carnegie	Savings and loan	412-276-2424
ICT Group, Inc.	Langhorne	Telemarketing	215-757-0200

	City	Business	Telephone
Interstate Hotels Co.	Pittsburgh	Hotel management	412-937-0600
Judge Group, Inc.	Bala Cynwyd	Consulting	610-667-7700
Knoll, Inc.	East Greenville	Office furniture	215-679-7991
Mastech Corp.	Oakdale	Information services	412-787-2100
NCO Group, Inc.	Blue Bell	Accounts receivable	610-832-1440
Old Guard Group, Inc.	Lancaster	Insurance	717-569-5361
ORBIT/FR, Inc.	Horsham	Wireless communications	215-674-5100
Pegasus Communications and Media Corp.	Radnor	Broadcasting	610-341-1801
Premier Research Worldwide, Ltd.	Philadelphia	Clinical research	215-972-0420
RMH Teleservices, Inc.	Bryn Mawr	Telemarketing	610-520-5300
SEEC, Inc.	Pittsburgh	Business software	412-682-4991
Telespectrum Worldwide, Inc.	King of Prussia	Telemarketing	610-962-5140
Triumph Group, Inc.	Wayne	Aircraft components	610-975-0420
Viropharma, Inc.	Malvern	Pharmaceuticals	610-651-0200
XLConnect Solutions, Inc.	Exton	Business consulting	610-458-5500

	City	*Business*	*Telephone*

Rhode Island

Access Solutions Int'l, Inc.	North Kingstown	Optical data storage	401-295-2691
Providence Journal Company	Providence	Television stations	401-277-7000

South Carolina

Community Capital Corporation	Greenwood	Bank holding company	864-941-8200
Emergent Group, Inc.	Greenville	Financial services	864-235-8056
Golf Trust of America, Inc.	Charleston	Real estate	803-768-8300
TearDrop Golf	Hilton Head Island	Golf clubs	803-686-4995

Tennessee

American Retirement Corp.	Brentwood	Elder-care services	615-221-2250
Birman Managed Care, Inc.	Cookeville	Health-care consulting	615-432-6532
Service Experts, Inc.	Nashville	Air-conditioning services	615-367-0003

Texas

Administaff, Inc.	Kingwood	Human resources	281-358-8986
Advance Paradigm, Inc.	Irving	Pharmacy services	214-830-6199

	City	Business	Telephone
Amarillo Biosciences, Inc.	Amarillo	Pharmaceuticals	806-376-1741
American General Hospitality Corp.	Dallas	Real estate	214-904-2000
American Pad & Paper Company	Dallas	Office paper products	214-733-6200
American Residential Services, Inc.	Houston	Air conditioning	713-706-6177
Apple Orthodontix, Inc.	Houston	Orthodontia	713-964-6882
AutoBond Acceptance Corp.	Austin	Financial services	512-435-7000
Brigham Exploration Company	Dallas	Oil and gas	214-360-9182
Carriage Services, Inc.	Houston	Death-care services	713-556-7400
CluckCorp International, Inc.	San Antonio	Restaurants	210-824-2496
Cornell Corrections, Inc.	Houston	Privatized prisons	713-623-0790
Costilla Energy, Inc.	Midland	Oil and gas	915-683-3092
Cross-Continent Auto Retailers, Inc.	Amarillo	Auto dealerships	806-374-8653
Dailey Petroleum Services Corp.	Conroe	Oil and gas	713-350-3399
Dal-Tile International, Inc.	Dallas	Ceramic tile	214-398-1411
Drilex International Inc.	Houston	Drilling equipment	713-937-8888
DSI Toys, Inc.	Houston	Toys	713-365-9900
DTM Corporation	Austin	Industrial equipment	512-339-2922

	City	*Business*	*Telephone*
DuPont Photomasks, Inc.	Round Rock	Photomasks	512-244-0024
Edge Petroleum Corp.	Houston	Oil and gas	713-654-8960
ErgoBilt, Inc.	Dallas	Office furniture	972-233-8504
First Sierra Financial, Inc.	Houston	Equipment leasing	713-221-8822
Genesis Energy L.P.	Houston	Oil pipeline	713-646-5466
Healthcor Holdings, Inc.	Dallas	Home health care	214-233-7744
Homegate Hospitality, Inc.	Dallas	Extended-stay hotels	214-863-1777
Houston Exploration Company	Houston	Oil and gas	713-652-2847
ILEX Oncology, Inc.	San Antonio	Cancer drugs	210-677-6080
IWL Communications, Inc.	Houston	Telecommunications	281-482-0289
IXC Communications, Inc.	Austin	Long-distance services	512-328-1112
Kevco, Inc.	Fort Worth	Building products	817-332-2758
Kitty Hawk, Inc.	Dallas	Air cargo management	214-456-2200
Medical Alliance, Inc.	Irvine	Surgical sites	214-580-8999
Metro Networks, Inc.	Houston	Television and radio	713-621-2800
Midcoast Energy Resources, Inc.	Houston	Pipeline construction	713-650-8900

	City	Business	Telephone
National-Oilwell, Inc.	Houston	Drilling equipment	713-960-5100
Nei Webworld, Inc.	Dallas	Printing	214-330-7273
Offshore Energy Development Corp.	The Woodlands	Natural gas	713-364-0033
Pagemart Wireless, Inc.	Dallas	Wireless messaging	214-750-5809
PalEx, Inc.	Houston	Pallets	713-626-9711
Paracelsus Healthcare Corp.	Houston	Acute-care hospitals	713-873-6623
Peerless Group, Inc.	Richardson	Digital imaging systems	214-497-5500
Prentiss Properties Trust, Inc.	Dallas	Real estate	214-761-1440
Prime Service, Inc.	Houston	Equipment rental	713-578-5600
ProMedCo Management Co.	Fort Worth	Practice management	817-335-5035
PSW Technologies, Inc.	Austin	Software services	512-343-6666
Rush Enterprises, Inc.	San Antonio	Trucking	210-829-1050
Rutherford-Moran Oil Corp.	Houston	Oil and gas	713-622-5555
Sabre Group Holdings, Inc.	Fort Worth	Travel reservations	817-931-7300
Santa Fe International Corp.	Dallas	Oil drilling	972-701-7300
Silverleaf Resorts, Inc.	Dallas	Time-share resorts	214-631-1166
Source Services Corp.	Dallas	Temporary staffing	214-385-3002

	City	Business	Telephone
Southwest Bancorp of Texas, Inc.	Houston	Bank holding company	713-235-8800
Stage Stores, Inc.	Houston	Apparel stores	713-667-5601
3DX Technologies, Inc.	Houston	Oil and gas	713-579-3398
Titan Exploration, Inc.	Midland	Oil and gas	915-682-6612
Travis Boats & Motors, Inc.	Austin	Boat retailer	512-250-8103

Utah

	City	Business	Telephone
NACT Telecommunications, Inc.	Orem	Telecommunications	801-225-6248
Nu Skin Asia Pacific, Inc.	Provo	Nutritional supplements	801-345-6100
Paradigm Medical Industries, Inc.	Salt Lake City	Ophthalmic surgery	801-977-8970
UroQuest Medical Corp.	Salt Lake City	Urological diagnosis	801-322-1554
Weider Nutrition International, Inc.	Salt Lake City	Nutritional supplements	801-975-5000

Virginia

	City	Business	Telephone
APACHE Medical Systems, Inc.	McLean	Health-care software	703-847-1400
CD-MAX, Inc.	Reston	CD technology	703-471-5755
Circuit City CarMax	Richmond	Used-car retailer	804-527-4000
Colonial Downs Holdings, Inc.	Providence Forge	Horse racing	804-966-7223
Cornerstone Realty Income Trust, Inc.	Richmond	Real estate	804-643-1761

	City	Business	Telephone
Deltek Systems, Inc.	McLean	Business software	703-734-8606
Dunn Computer Corp.	Sterling	Computers	703-450-0400
LCC International, Inc.	Arlington	Wireless communications	703-351-6666
Marathon Financial Corp.	Winchester	Bank holding company	540-869-6600
MAXIMUS, Inc.	McLean	Government services	703-734-4200
Metro Information Services, Inc.	Virginia Beach	Consulting	757-486-1900
MLC Holdings, Inc.	Reston	Equipment leasing	703-834-5710
Objective Communications, Inc.	Chantilly	Video communications	703-227-3000
On-Site Sourcing, Inc.	Arlington	Facilities management	703-276-1123
Primus Telecommunications Group, Inc.	McLean	Long distance service	703-848-4625
Telco Communications Group, Inc.	Chantilly	Long distance service	703-631-5600
Template Software, Inc.	Dulles	Business software	703-318-1000
Trigon Healthcare, Inc.	Richmond	Managed health care	804-354-7000
UOL Publishing, Inc.	Falls Church	On-line education	703-533-7500
Versatility, Inc.	Fairfax	Telemarketing	703-591-2900

	City	Business	Telephone
Xybernaut Corp.	Fairfax	Mobile computer systems	703-631-6925

Washington

	City	Business	Telephone
Advanced Radio Telecom Corp.	Bellevue	Wireless telecom	206-688-8700
Aftermarket Technology Corp.	Federal Way	Drive-train products	206-838-0346
Alternative Living Services, Inc.	Brookfield	Assisted living	414-789-9565
Amazon.Com, Inc.	Seattle	On-line bookstore	206-622-2335
Apex PC Solutions, Inc.	Woodinville	Switching systems	206-402-9393
ARIS Corp.	Seattle	Computer training	206-433-2081
Cell Therapeutics, Inc.	Seattle	Cancer drugs	206-282-7100
Gargoyles, Inc.	Kent	Glasses	206-872-6100
Gentle Dental Service Corp.	Vancouver	Dental practice mgmt.	360-750-7975
go2net, Inc.	Seattle	Internet information	206-447-1595
Microvision, Inc.	Seattle	Information display	206-623-7055
Multicom Publishing, Inc.	Seattle	Consumer software	206-622-5530
Multiple Zones International, Inc.	Bellevue	Microcomputer products	206-603-2400
Omniquip International, Inc.	Port Washington	Material handlers	414-284-5571
SeaMed Corp.	Redmond	Medical instruments	206-867-1818

	City	*Business*	*Telephone*
West Virginia			
Advance Financial Bancorp	Wellsburg	Bank holding company	304-737-3531
Valley National Gases, Inc.	Wheeling	Industrial gases	304-232-1541
Wyoming			
Casull Arms Corp.	Afton	Firearms	307-886-0200

Source: IPO Data Systems (http://www.ipodata.com)

APPENDIX C:
FURTHER READING

PETER LYNCH

Beating the Street
by Peter Lynch and John Rothchild
Published by Fireside/Simon & Schuster
Publication date: May 1, 1994
ISBN: 0671891634
Paperback: $12.50

Learn to Earn: A Beginner's Guide to the Basics of Investing and Business
by Peter Lynch and John Rothchild
Published by Fireside/Simon & Schuster
Publication date: January 1, 1996
ISBN: 0684811634
Paperback: $13.00

One Up on Wall Street: How to Use What You Already Know to Make Money in the Market
by Peter Lynch and John Rothchild
Published by Penguin USA
Publication date: February 1, 1990
ISBN: 0140127925
Paperback: $12.50

WARREN BUFFETT

Buffett: The Making of an American Capitalist
by Roger Lowenstein
Published by Doubleday
Publication date: September 1, 1996
ISBN: 0385484917
Paperback: $14.95

Buffettology: The Previously Unexplained Techniques That Have Made Warren Buffett the World's Most Famous Investor
by Mary Buffett and David Clark
Published by Scribner
Publication date: November 1, 1997
ISBN: 0684837137
Hardcover: $27.50

The Midas Touch: The Strategies That Have Made Warren Buffett "America's Pre-eminent Investor"
by John Train
Published by HarperCollins (paper)
Publication date: June 1, 1988
ISBN: 0060915005
Paperback: $12.50

Of Permanent Value: The Story of Warren Buffett
by Andrew Kilpatrick
Published by Andy Kilpatrick Publishing Empire
Publication date: October 1, 1996
ISBN: 0964190516
Hardcover: $30.00

Warren Buffett: The Good Guy of Wall Street
by Andrew Kilpatrick
Published by Donald I. Fine
Publication date: January 1, 1995
ISBN: 155611432X
Paperback: $14.95

Warren Buffett Speaks: Wit and Wisdom from the World's Greatest Investor
by Warren Buffett and Janet C. Lowe
Published by John Wiley & Sons
Publication date: April 1, 1997
ISBN: 047116996X
Hardcover: $16.95

The Warren Buffett Way: Investment Strategies of the World's Greatest Investor
by Robert G. Hagstrom
Published by John Wiley & Sons
Publication date: November 1, 1995
ISBN: 0471132985
Paperback: $16.95

OTHER

Beating the Dow: A High Return, Low-Risk Method for Investing in the Dow Jones Industrial Stocks with as Little as $5,000 Dollars
by Michael O'Higgins with John Downes.
Harper Perennial, 1992
Paperback $13.00
ISBN 0-06-098404-X